Thomas Maguire

An Essay on the Platonic Idea

Thomas Maguire

An Essay on the Platonic Idea

ISBN/EAN: 9783742826565

Manufactured in Europe, USA, Canada, Australia, Japa

Cover: Foto ©Klaus-Uwe Gerhardt /pixelio.de

Manufactured and distributed by brebook publishing software (www.brebook.com)

Thomas Maguire

An Essay on the Platonic Idea

AN ESSAY

ON

THE PLATONIC IDEA.

BY

THOMAS MAGUIRE, A.M.,

OF TRINITY COLLEGE, DUBLIN; AND OF LINCOLN'S INN, BARRISTER-AT-LAW.

Τί δέ; ὁ τἀναντία τούτων ἡγούμενος τί τι αὐτὸ καλὸν καὶ δυνάμενος καθορᾶν καὶ αὐτὸ καὶ τὰ ἐκείνου μετέχοντα, καὶ οὔτε τὰ μετέχοντα αὐτὸ οὔτε αὐτὸ τὰ μετέχοντα ἡγούμενος, ὕπαρ ἢ ὄναρ αὖ καὶ οὗτος δοκεῖ σοι ζῆν; καὶ μάλα, ἔφη, ὄναρ.—PLATO, *Repub.* v. 476, C—D.

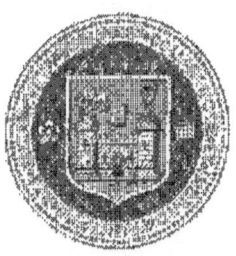

LONDON:
LONGMANS, GREEN, READER, AND DYER.
DUBLIN: W. M'GEE, NASSAU-STREET.
1860.

PREFACE.

'Εγὼ δὲ τίνων εἰμί; τῶν ἡδέως μὲν ἂν ἐλεγχθέντων, εἴ τι μὴ ἀληθὲς λέγω, ἡδέως δ' ἂν ἐλεγξάντων, εἴ τίς τι μὴ ἀληθὲς λέγοι, οὐκ ἀηδέστερον μέντ' ἂν ἐλεγχθέντων ἢ ἐλεγξάντων.—PLATO, *Gorg.* 458, A.

THE following Essay results from an independent study of Plato. The diversities of critics suggested the possibility of making Plato explain himself. The notion was accordingly carried out in its integrity, without any foregone conclusion, and without, in the first instance, any view to publication. But neither during the preparatory studies, nor after publication was resolved on, have any materials been used, save the text of Plato without note or comment, and the scattered hints of Aristotle.

The propriety of the exception in favour of Aristotle will be at once apparent. To reject Aristotelian tradition would be to set aside a contemporary witness, with the fullest means of information, and all the will to use them. Aristotle was for twenty years intimate with Plato. Aristotle published his report, which unhappily is lost, of the most transcendental part of Plato's lectures, side by side with the reports by other pupils of Plato on the same subject. Misconceptions on Aristotle's part were, consequently, liable to immediate correction by writers who had heard and reported the very same course. Aristotle's inquiring disposition is shown by anecdote, as well as by the universal range of his works. We know Plato's lofty conception of the duties of a teacher. We know his estimate of all written composition: the very best of compositions was senseless and dull, when contrasted with the intelligent *vivâ voce* answer elicited by a skilful cross-examiner. Unless, therefore, we maintain that Plato *would* not answer the questions which his method must have taught Aristotle to put, it is almost certain that Aristotle must have understood Platonism.

Further, no man in modern times can pretend to the same *familiarity* with metaphysical speculation as either Plato or Aristotle. With us, owing to the authority of Christianity and the preponderance of views which are supposed to be Baconian, metaphysics have sunk into a very subordinate position.

They have degenerated into either an academic exercise, or a convenient vehicle for theological discussion. Even the upper class of the general reading public takes no notice of metaphysics until they savour of theology. The Dry Light must be softened by a coloured medium.

With the Greek it was different. The Greek intellect was too vigorous to do without a consistent scheme of life and conduct. Aristotle, then, as well as Plato, must have heard nearly every possible phase of metaphysical opinion argued out by advocates who felt that they were fighting for their most cherished principles of life and thought. It could, therefore, have been no want of metaphysical training, which prevented Aristotle from knowing what Plato meant.

Besides, Platonism was not a novelty. Plato was an eclectic. He amalgamated in one systematic whole the current theories of his day. It was, as we shall see, a principle of Plato's, that elements remain unaltered by composition. But, as Aristotle was well acquainted with the elements, their reappearance in a compound form could have presented no peculiar difficulty. For these reasons, Aristotle's competency as a witness will hardly be disputed.

But, in making use of Aristotle's notices, a certain distinction must be kept in view. Every criticism indicates the opinion of the critic, as well as the opinion of the person criticized; but every criticism which deserves the name must be directed from a determinate position. We shall see that Aristotle's objections have their basis in his point of divergence from Plato's line of thought. We must, accordingly, expect to find that the Platonic fragments have been somewhat affected by the pressure of the system in which they are imbedded. Subject to the above qualification, Aristotle's comments tally in a remarkable manner with the results obtained from the Platonic text.

The points which the Writer seeks to prove are two. The first is, that the Idea and Platonism are identical; that the Idea, consequently, cannot be removed from the organic whole of Plato's Philosophy, without the total destruction of the system. The second is, that Plato rejects the existence of matter, as an objective *tertium quid*, between the psychic principle and the Idea. The second proposition is strictly a consequence of the first; but its prominence in modern speculation may, perhaps, justify its separate position.

PREFACE.

When the Essay was nearly re-written, Mr. Grote's "Plato" appeared. As it would have been the height of folly and presumption to bring out what professed to be an original view of Plato side by side with Mr. Grote's, the Essay was laid by, and Mr. Grote's book repeatedly perused. The Writer has, however, seen no reason to change his views. The text has accordingly been left unaltered; and Mr. Grote's opinions will be noticed in the Notes. But, as it was the splendid chapter on Socrates in the History of Greece, to which the Writer owes his first conviction that mental science was not mere verbiage, he must, without laying claim to the destructive powers of the Eleatic stranger, be allowed to say, Μή με οἶον πατραλοίαν ὑπολάβῃς γίγνεσθαί τινα. Τί δή; Τὸν τοῦ πατρὸς Παρμενίδου λόγον ἀναγκαῖον ἡμῖν ἀμυνομένοις ἔσται βασανίζειν.

Mr. Grote's propositions are two. The first is, that the two currents of Platonic speculation—negative cross-examination, and affirmative dogmatism—are distinct and independent of each other.—"Plato," vol. i., p. 270. The affirmative theory "has its roots, *aliunde*, being neither generated nor adopted, with a view to reconcile the contradictions, or elucidate the obscurities, which the negative Elenchus has exposed." Vol. i., p. 292. The second is, that the Platonic "theory of objective Ideas, separate and absolute, which the commentators often announce as if it cleared up all difficulties, not only clears up none, but introduces fresh ones belonging to itself." Ib., p. 270.

With respect to the language of the Essay, considerable difficulty has been felt. The interest of the sensual school lies wholly in purism. The sensualist, by using the simplest words, not only justly enhances his fame as a writer, but strengthens his position. The spiritualist, on the contrary, cannot take up an ordinary word, which may not be put in evidence against his case. He is, consequently, reduced to the alternative either of citing testimony, which tells in part against himself, or of having recourse to metaphor. Of the two dangers, the Writer has chosen the former. No word, save one, has been employed, which is not current in the philosophy of the present day.

The word noetic has been employed on the authority of Coleridge. It is more tractable than the cognate noematic, in use with the English Platonists. It is, besides, more correct; it calls attention to the outward process, rather than to the internal result, of intuition. Further, there is no other word which does not mislead: rational and intelligible have a direct subjective reference, which is the very thing which it is intended to eliminate. One Platonic word will perhaps be pardoned,

Πελοποννασιστὶ λαλιῦμες·
Δωρίσδεν δ' ἔξεστι, δοκῶ, τοῖς Δωριέεσσιν.

The text will consist of the results of the investigation thrown into the form of a connected statement. The references will be found in the Notes, with occasionally a few remarks, to justify the process by which the modernised equivalent was extracted from the Platonic formula. In the note on the word Idea, all the passages containing it which the Writer could find will be cited. But, as the plan of the work forbade the use of any external aid, the Reader may rest assured that any passage which is cited was actually worked in. The plan will perhaps, likewise, palliate any omissions which the student of Plato may discover.

CONTENTS.

		PAGE.
PREFACE,		iii
I.	THE PROBLEM OF PHILOSOPHY,	1
II.	THE SENSUAL HYPOTHESIS,	6
III.	SUPERSENSUOUS ENTITIES,	34
IV.	OBJECTIVE ENTITIES,	44
V.	THE OBJECTIVE UNIVERSE,	55
VI.	PARTICIPATION,	74
VII.	THE DEMIURGE OF THE TIMÆUS,	84
VIII.	JUSTICE,	111
IX.	IMMORTALITY,	152
NOTES,		159

AN ESSAY

on

THE PLATONIC IDEA.

I.

THE PROBLEM OF PHILOSOPHY.

οὐχ ἱερήιον οὐδὲ βοείην
Ἀρνύσθην, ἅ,τε ποσσὶν ἀέθλια γίγνεται ἀνδρῶν,
Ἀλλὰ περὶ ψυχῆς θέον.—Hom. *Il.* xxii. 159, *sq.*

SPECULATIVE thought has always assumed one of two forms; it has always been either dogmatic or sceptical. Dogmatism and scepticism both embody the same fact, but their respective points of view are different. The fact with which either form deals is, that there is *something* always to be said on both sides of every speculative question. After two thousand years' discussion the criterion of right and wrong, and the grounds both of mathematical demonstration and of its dependent, the higher physical science, are still under argument. But, as truth cannot rise above its source, it is obvious that the laws of the physical and moral worlds contain the elements of anarchy. Scepticism may indeed be silenced by the fruits of allegiance; but the spirit of disloyalty is not the less real. Dogmatism and scepticism are therefore, now as heretofore, the two possible forms of speculative thought.

Of these, the dogmatist holds that, as a general rule, one side of the question preponderates in fact, whether that side be affirmative or negative. The business of the dogmatist is to discover on which side the balance lies; and the final result is either certainty or probability, according as the arguments are found to lie really all on one side, opposition being only *primâ facie*, or as a real minority of opposing arguments is outvoted, but not annihilated, by a majority of reasons large or small. Certainty and probability, therefore, are to the dogmatist the modes of truth.

The sceptic, on the other hand, alleges that the strife between the two sides is internecine. In his opinion, the positive and negative arguments, when traced to their ground principles, must always equate; and the final result is zero.* The term truth, therefore, may denote the equilibrium of the equal and opposite forces, in which case it has no positive value; or it may denote the possibility of conceiving one side of the equation cancelled, not in fact, but in

---

* The sceptical zero means, not a purely negative *process*, which is a contradiction, but a purely negative *result*.

thought. In the latter case, the term truth may mean that we are able to concentrate our attention on a portion of a fact without regarding the remainder. The term truth may, therefore, denote either negative mental equilibrium, or positive one-sidedness, but nothing more. But the answer of the sceptic, as well as of the dogmatist, assumes that the question, What is truth ? has been raised. The cardinal problem of philosophy, on either hypothesis, is therefore to determine what is meant by truth.

For present purposes, truth may be defined as that mental state, or sum of mental states, to which the possessor attaches his final opinion, solely in consequence of a special state of the cognitive faculty relatively to its supposed object. The solution of the problem must, therefore, be sought in that relation. To the question so conceived, one of two answers must be given :—The final state of thought must be either wholly a product of the senses, or it must derive some of its constituents from a source which is supersensuous. The former is the answer of sensualism, the latter of spiritualism.

But the classification of thought into dogmatism and scepticism, and into sensualism and spiritualism, may be a cross division. Psychologically, a sceptic may or may not allow that the supersensuous is a factor of the mental sum, and so may the dogmatist; subjectively, therefore, sceptics and dogmatists may belong to either school. But on the point of objective existence their views necessarily diverge. Objective existence the dogmatist either asserts or denies. Objective existence the sceptic neither asserts nor denies: on his principles, he can find no subject with which to begin his proposition—*à fortiori*, he cannot find a predicate to end it. 0 is a useful expression of $x-x$; but $0=0$, save as a blank form to be subsequently filled, is totally unmeaning. All sides may, accordingly, take part in the psychological debate; as the psychologist deals with mental facts, and not with ultra-mental inferences: but when the ontological question arises, the sceptic drops out; his constituents are so evenly divided, that he dare not vote. Psychology, therefore, cannot ignore either sensualism or spiritualism; and psychology is either the basis of ontology or the chasm in which it disappears.

Subject, however, to the distinction between dogmatism and scepticism, the two forms of psychology are sensualism and spiritualism. A sensualist holds that every notion, however apparently remote from any mode of sensation, may be ultimately resolved into the concrete presentations of the different senses, although in its present shape its ingredients may escape detection; that mind adds nothing to the sensuous material upon which it works; that the conception soul or spirit is an abstraction, obtained by detaching in thought all the conditions which render existence not only possible, but even intelligible; that the meaning of the higher abstractions is most properly seen in their application to the immediate objects of the senses, and that all other usages are metaphorical, and less real.

A spiritualist, on the other hand, maintains that spirit, even psychologically, is the primary reality; that spirit is the indissoluble combination of reason and emotive energy, the united aspect of which is personality; that such notions as unity, identity, substance, &c., are not abstractions derived from the sensuous concrete substance called matter, but properly from spiritual reality; that, if spiritual reality be denied, these terms are, strictly speaking, unintelligible; that to explain the facts which the spiritualist alleges by an extension of the process of abstraction as applied to sensuous materials, is literally to explain the substance by the shadow; and, lastly, that the proper sense of the higher terms of psychology is to be sought in the facts and operations of spirit, and not in their sensuous or material analogues.

Of this latter school of thought Plato is the main prop; and this Essay attempts to give as a connected whole,[1] his answer to the problem of philosophy.

II.

THE SENSUAL HYPOTHESIS.

*Οἱ δ' ὑπ' ὀπωρινὸν Βορέης φορέησιν ἀκάνθαι
Ἂμ πεδίον, πυκιναὶ δὲ πρὸς ἀλλήλῃσιν ἔχονται.—*
Hom. *Od.* v. 328-9.

THE senses contribute largely to our mental furniture. Their deliverances, even on the showing of the spiritualist, are not of necessity delusions.[1] The relation, moreover, between the senses and their objects, gives rise to the notion property, and the aggregate of rights and duties, social, legal, and political, founded thereon.[2] Language, too, appears to have been, in Plato's opinion, framed in accordance with the views of sensualism.[3] These facts, coupled with the superior simplicity of the sensual hypothesis, fairly cast on its impugnant the *onus* of proof. The spiritualist must expose the weakness of sensualism, before the counter scheme be called in to give its version of the facts of consciousness. The sensual hypothesis, accordingly, must be examined first.

The sensual hypothesis is, that sensation and the raw material of truth are identical. Now, of sensations relatively to the cognitive faculty, two assertions, and two only, are possible—their presence, or their absence. But sensations are of two kinds: they are either actual impressions, conveyed through the percipient organs; or they are the counterparts of impressions depicted in the imagination⁴ and memory. Sensations of the former class are more or less consciously referred to a special state of the bodily organism, as their immediate antecedent. Sensations of the latter class are referred to a state of mind as their antecedent; or, correctly speaking, as another connected portion of the same united whole.⁵ But, in either case, sensations involve a reference to reality of some kind or other. Relatively to the mode of entrance, the former class is mediate, and the latter immediate. Relatively to the *quantum* of reality, the former class is, to borrow Sir W. Hamilton's apt terms, presentative, and the latter representative. The former are the originals, of which the latter are copies.

If sensation and the field of mental discovery be coextensive, three theories of truth are possible; or, strictly speaking, two main theories, the latter of which branches into two species. If truth and sensation be convertible, truth must be either the sensations themselves, or their relations. Again, these latter may be either primary relations, between sensations themselves; or secondary relations, between sensations and their verbal signs. Truth, according to the first theory, deals with sensations in their primary relation to the subject; according to the second, with sensations in their primary relation to each other, and in their secondary relation to the subject; according to the third, with sensations (including their relations to each other and to the subject) in their tertiary relation to the subject in the shape of words. In the first form the *quantum* of sensation is at its maximum; in the second, at its minimum; in the third, at an intermediate degree. There is no more concrete sensuous fact than sensation, appealing as it may to all the senses; and no more abstract sign than the literal symbol, appealing, as it does, but to one sense only. The third form presupposes the first, of which it is the antithesis, but the converse does not hold. The second form presupposes both, but the converse does not hold. This arrangement, which, it is obvious, is exhaustive, is, as will be seen, an example of Plato's universal mode of thought.

According to the first variety of the sensual hypothesis, truth is the presence of one or more sensations of either kind. Truth will therefore be opposed to the utter absence of sensations of either kind. All states of mind which deal with sensuous impressions, or their fainter counterparts in the imagination and memory, are in possession of truth. All other mental states are to be imputed to the mind itself, which weaves its fabric aloof from the realities of sense. This is the first form of the sensual hypothesis.

Should this form be rejected, and truth be notwithstanding confined to sensuous states of mind, truth must lie in the grouping of sensations as like or unlike, and must be sought in the similarity or dissimilarity of two sets of sensations, more or less complex: since, if truth and sensation be partly identical, and truth is not the bare presence of sensation as opposed to its absence, truth must lie in the due joinder of sensations according to their relations *inter se*. On the same hypothesis, a falsity is a case of mistaken identity or diversity. The logical organon of the theory is comparison, with its subsidiary instruments, abstraction and composition. This is the second form of the sensual hypothesis.

Or, finally, rejecting the view that truth lies wholly in the relations of sensations *inter se*, but retaining both the raw material and the logical instrument of the former theory, their product will not receive the stamp of truth until the whole of the result be connoted by a verbal sign which specifies its chief ingredients. Truth will, on this hypothesis, lie in the relation between a complex sensation and the verbal synthesis which registers its elements; and this is the third and last variety of the sensual hypothesis.

The three varieties of the sensual hypothesis differ, not, of necessity, in their psychology, but in their views of the matter of judgments; and, as each theory rests on the same psychological basis, each in succession incurs the difficulties of its predecessor in addition to its own. To avoid repetition, however, the examination of each variety will deal with special difficulties only. Strictly speaking, if the first form of the hypothesis break down, the two which rest on it must share its fate; but Plato, in discussing the two latter varieties, makes certain concessions, which he afterwards recalls, as contradictory to the principles of sensualism.

1. *The first Form of the Hypothesis.*

The first form of the sensual hypothesis branches out into three varieties. The first variety is the view of common sense wholly unmodified by reflection. It asserts that the sum of the facts of perception is an aggregate of three distinct things: the percipient subject, the perceived object, and the percipient process by which the former perceives the latter. The second variety is the view of common sense more or less modified by reflection. It admits that the object is to a greater or less extent modified in the percipient process. The third variety is the complete antithesis of the first, and is the view of reflection carried out to its legitimate conclusions. It asserts that the three items of perception are not three integers, but really three fractions of the one integer. Logical analysis, for more convenient treatment, supposes the integer to be so divided, and confers upon each fraction a fictitious individuality, which exists only in and during thought. In strictness, the three items—subject, object and process—are but abstract terms, which denote the same fact viewed from different points.

The first theory is the logical basis of the other

two. A person might, and the majority of people do, hold the first, without any reference to the two last; and the third might be held without reference to the second; but the second cannot be maintained without more or less reference to the third and first, since the second is a compromise between the two extremes. This arrangement is another instance of Plato's universal mode of thought.

The two first theories need not detain us long. It is a fact that sensations vary, not only in animals of different orders; not only in animals of the same order, but also in the same individual at different times.[*] Modern experiment has added, in different parts of the same body at the same time.[†] This fact directly overturns the first supposition, and indirectly the second. For, reflection once admitted, where is the line to be drawn?

The third variety of the sensual hypothesis is very important; it contains Plato's view of the outer aspect of physical causation, and is similar to the generally received modern theory of the mutual relation of phenomena. Plato does not except to the notion as it stands, but denies that it can be derived from the sensual hypothesis. His rationale of sensation is as follows:—

The senses are, in his concrete language, the instruments of perception; in abstract terms, the percipient organs are some of the antecedents of sensation. The antecedents of sensation may be, accordingly, divided into two classes—the organic and the extra-organic—

and the junction of these produces the actual presentation. Sensations may therefore be considered either in relation to their immediate antecedents, or with regard to the characteristics of their completed phase.[8]

In relation to their antecedents, presentations are the effect of contact between the organ and its object. This is the general rule—subject, however, to the notable exceptions of dreaming and delirium; but in every case the impression is presented as one homogeneous whole, or resultant, which cannot be resolved into its component forces.[9] And this brings us to the actual characteristics of the completed sensation.

The impression is, as now said, one homogeneous whole. In the sensuous presentation, the organ and the object are not severally distinguishable. Of the sum total of perception, we cannot appropriate the items to the organic and the extra-organic contributors, respectively. We do not perceive the organ and object to be either out of, or in one another: this is true as a matter of fact.[10]

Reasoning, also, gives the same result. The final phase of the presentation through each organ is unique in character; colour, for example, is not sound, and so on. The unique presentation is, accordingly, said to be the object, *id circa quod*, of that sense. Thus, we see colours, and colour is the object of the eye. Now, if the eye be an object of vision, it must present colour. But the second colour (the eye) implies a second eye, and so to infinity; similarly, the other senses. The organ and the object cannot, therefore, be presented either as halves of the same whole or as whole and part alternately.[11]

Combining the two relations of sensuous states, every sensation may be described as an impression more or less transient, as a longer or shorter period of transition. Now, the notion transition yields to analysis the following correlative, but not co-ordinate elements: Transition involves the several notions of an antecedent passing into its consequent, through a stage of indifference. Comparing these notions, Consequent of necessity involves Antecedent; but it is not necessarily true that Antecedent is nothing but Antecedent, for it may sustain other relations: the notion Indifference, of necessity, involves both Consequent and Antecedent; but the converse is not necessary. We find, accordingly, that of these notions Antecedent is prior to Consequent, and both to Indifference, in the logical order of thought. But the notions Antecedent and Consequent stand to each other in the relation of logical contraries. Hence, Plato's law of phenomena: Contraries are brought into being out of Contraries. This means, in modern language, that the law of physical causation is a relation of antecedence and consequence; that the aggregate of sensible phenomena is a cycle of production and decay.[12]

The several distinctions—Antecedent, Consequent, and Indifference—appear sharp enough. But

the clearness of the analysis is more verbal than real.
The notions Antecedent, Consequent, and Indifference, are essentially relative—relative not only *inter se*, but also with regard to the antecedents and consequents of other orders. Every antecedent is a consequent relatively to the preceding link in the chain; and so, conversely, the consequent.[15] But the relativity of phenomena does not stop here. Every distinct sequent in each order may be considered as a phenomenon, which yields on resolution, as before, *its* complete set of sequents; and each of these may be subjected to a fresh analysis, which presents a similar result, and so on to infinity. Hence the Heracleitan doctrine, that all things are in a state of flux. The doctrine is not that a state of flux is a superficial aspect of phenomena, which involves a substantial residuum. The doctrine is, that flux and existence are coextensive, and properly, not metaphorically, identical. Flux is not an abstract description of all things; all-things, on the contrary, is an abstract description of flux. Flux is the real essence; all-things, its mental analysis and synthesis. With this doctrine Plato does not quarrel, save as a statement of the *whole* truth. The doctrine of Heracleitus is true; but it is not, in Plato's opinion, the whole truth.

Such being, in Plato's eyes, the meaning of the sensual hypothesis, his criticism is obvious. Every sensation is a portion of an infinite sequence, which exists only during the collision of opposite sequents, antecedent and consequent, and of which it is the inevitable result. Such words as Permanence and Unity denote merely that the antagonism of contraries, antecedent and consequent, is apparently, but not really, prolonged by the intervention of a new train of sequents, each infinitely resolvable as before.[14] The so-called subject—the percipient psychic principle—is essentially flux; the so-called object is essentially flux, and nothing more. All sensations—all modes of consciousness—are but ripples on the stream. That the law of antecedence and consequence binds sensible phenomena Plato admits, but he denies that it can be evolved from the sensual hypothesis. Strictly speaking, on that hypothesis the bare observation of physical sequence is, in Plato's opinion, impossible. A sequence involves succession; succession involves number; and number, unity.[15] Now, unity implies at least a provisional nucleus of permanence somewhere; but analysis shows that every member of each series is, in the strictest sense, infinitely resolvable. Analysis sublimates into flux the *quasi*-permanence of the subject, of the organ, and of the extra-organic object: subject, organ, and object, alike melt away in the same potent solvent. In the absence of unity, the percipient subject is an indefinite series of sequences, infinitely resolvable, as before. Man is literally the creature of the moment—a chance formation of drift. On its most favourable showing, the hypothesis confines reality to the perception of transition; but, in strictness, there can be neither transition to observe, nor any one to observe it. In the absence of unity, there is neither subject nor object, neither permanence nor transition, neither reality nor semblance. The result is nihilism, the negation of metaphysical substance and of every consequent result.

In brief, Plato's argument is: the notion transition is real and true, though not coextensive with all reality and with all truth; but the basis of transition is unity, for which the sensual hypothesis cannot account. The sensual hypothesis, therefore, is not true. The same criticism underlies his subsequent examination of the other forms of the same hypothesis.

The negation of metaphysical unity involves, in Plato's opinion, the negation of phenomenal semblance.[16] Hence the sensual hypothesis and consciousness clash *adversis frontibus*. The second form of the hypothesis, accordingly, postulates a unifying faculty in the subject, without supposing a corresponding unity in the object.[17] Some framework is necessary to give the object at least psychological cohesion. The objective indefinite must be run through a subjective mould.

2. *The second Form of the Hypothesis.*

Truth, we have seen, cannot be the presence merely of a single sensation, presentation, or representative. But truth, being *ex hypothesi* wholly confined to sensuous states, may be a relation either between the objects of the several senses; or between a presentation and a representation; or between two representations, more or less complex.

At the risk of appearing tedious, it must be repeated that this is another instance of Plato's universal mode of thought. The third variety is the direct antithesis of the first, upon the basis of which it rests. The second, as usual, partakes of both extremes, and presupposes them; but the converse does not hold.

The first variety may be summarily dismissed. Each sense is idiopathic, and resembles the other organs only in being an antecedent *per se*. The relation, therefore, between these objects must be diversity, and all judgments would take the negative form—Colour is not sound.[18] The claims of the latter two competitors remain to be decided.

According to the theory, the mind is a receptacle[19] which cannot enlarge its contents by any internal manipulation. It can merely tabulate what is already in store, and all mental activity is confined to arrangement exclusively.

Every arrangement ultimately rests on similarity and difference. According to the theory, arrangement engrosses all mental activity; truth, therefore, must be the perception of the agreement or disagreement of sensations of both kinds, either single or in groups. The organon of the theory, accordingly, is comparison; and the product must be tested by the canons of identity and contradiction. All affirmative judgments must take the form, A is A; all negative judgments must take the other form, A is not B; and all judgments which do not violate these two canons must be absolutely true. But, as no judgment can possibly violate either without an obvious contradiction, a false judgment is impossible.

For example, the presentation horse is presented as horse; and the concept horse is conceived as horse; and while presented or conceived, as such, cannot be any other percept, or concept, save horse. Affirmative judgments, on analysis, are found to assert that horse is perceived or conceived as horse. Negative judgments, on the other hand, assert that horse is perceived or conceived as not, say, ox; the latter term of comparison being assumed as known, that is, either perceived or conceived. Both terms must be known; for it is obvious that we cannot compare a thing with pure zero. Such a symbol as —— is ——, or —— is not ——, has no meaning, save as a skeleton form of judgments. Both terms, therefore, being given as known, each term must be known as either similar or dissimilar to the other. In either case we *eo ipso* predicate their respective similarity or dissimilarity, either mentally or verbally. No one, therefore, can think a falsity; and the distinction of judgments into true and false is perfectly unmeaning."

If we shift our ground, and confine truth to conformity between an impression and its copy, the same difficulty recurs. The copy A is conceived to resemble the original A; and the predication of such resemblance is a mental necessity; and so, *mutatis mutandis*, negative judgments. The laws of identity and contradiction come in as before."[1] In other words, things, to be compared, must be known ; and if known, need not be compared.

It is plain that, if the complete similarity of two concepts be not truth, the partial similarity of two concepts is not truth. Concepts which as wholes are partially similar, are completely similar in the special points of mutual resemblance. Plato accordingly excludes, for these and other reasons, all deductive sciences, which rest on the basis of postulate and definition, from the category of pure truth.

Mathematical science, as he conceived it, is a deductive process, which has for its basis a compound proposition. The ground proposition contains two heterogeneous elements, the laws of quantity, and the most attenuated abstraction of sensible phenomena. The two elements combined by way of postulate, become the definition. Mathematical correctness is, therefore, conformity to the ground proposition from which we originally started; but the validity of the hypothesis *per se* is not within the scope of mathematics. Geometry, for example, does not profess to discuss the nature of pure space. Yet, as mathematical conclusions are true, without any consideration of time past or future as such, mathematical truth approaches most nearly of human sciences to real truth, as Plato conceived it—to truth wholly free from any material relation. But the constituents of mathematics, which give it its high position, are not derived from any process of comparison. Mathematical certainty, therefore, as far as it rests on postulate and definition, is not the purest form of truth.[22]

The position of physical science is somewhat similar. Physical science, is like mathematics, a complex whole, made up of heterogeneous elements. These elements are certain modes of number, and the matter of sensible phenomena in subordination thereto. Physical science, therefore, so far as it is subject to numerical law, is of the nature of mathematics, although in one respect, to be afterwards considered, it in Plato's opinion ranks above mathematics. But, with regard to the outer aspect of physics, the business of the natural philosopher is to observe the relations of phenomena. These relations are of two kinds, simultaneity and succession. The result of such observation is a power of predicting and of controlling the future.[23]

Now, it cannot surely be alleged that Plato's conception of physical observation could be at all enlarged by the most minute acquaintance with the process of modern experiment. Experiment presents to observation sensations which are either strange or familiar. If the sensation be strange, the difficulties of the first form of the sensual hypothesis at once attach. The sensation, to be known, must be unified; and unification the sensual hypothesis cannot, in Plato's opinion, explain. If the sensation be

THE SENSUAL HYPOTHESIS. 21

familiar, the difficulties are doubled; there are two unifications to be accounted for; and verification, the process of comparison, can yield no aid. It is certain, then, that if Plato refused to place his conception of physical sequence in the highest grade of knowledge, he most assuredly would not have been induced to alter his opinion by the most brilliant discoveries of modern experiment.[14] Plato would admit the dignity and the utility of modern physics; he would acknowledge their correctness in terms which would satisfy their most zealous votary; but they would never reach, in his opinion, the farthest degree of certainty our mind may attain. Plato saw in a spot of mud[15] the very same difficulties, neither more nor less, which he would see in the law of gravity in its most precise expression, and in its cosmical extent. Either object would elicit exactly the same thought, and similar problems would meet with similar solutions. Modern physics, so far as they are regulated by the laws of quantity, he would class with mathematics in their higher aspects, and in this shape he would have held them to be a strong confirmation of his views. But physics, so far as they are not regulated by the laws of quantity, would, in his opinion, constitute a branch of psychology. The peculiar matter of sensible phenomena, apart from the laws of quantity, correspond, as will be shown, to the secondary qualities of modern metaphysics.[16] It is obvious, therefore, that physical science can give no rationale of certainty which is not exposed to the difficulties on account of which Plato rejected the sensual hypothesis. Nothing, consequently, can be more absurd than to pit Bacon against Plato. The Baconian method took for granted that the sensuous material of perception was already unified, without inquiring how or where."⁷ But the nature and origin of unity was the point at issue between Plato and the sensual school.

The objections which the process of comparison suggests are fatal to conceptualism as an exposition of the highest certainty. All concepts, ranging in complexity from the abstract idea of Locke to the smallest fragment which marks a feeling of similarity, are representative, and as such involve a comparison with their originals. The old difficulty recurs: terms are compared because they are known, not known because they are compared. If there be unity in the original sensation, it need not be sought in the copy; and unless there be unity in the original, it cannot be found in the copy. But these objections, however fatal to comparison as the organon of objective truth, do not affect its uses as a means to subjective consistency. The value of comparison in this latter capacity is fully recognised by Plato.[28]

In brief, the process of comparison presupposes unity, if not in the object, at least in the subject; if the object-matter of the sensation be in itself indefinite, its unification must come from within. But if there be unity in the subject, the sensual hypothesis is not thoroughgoing, and is therefore not true;

and if the sensual hypothesis be true, there can be no unity in the subject. In itself, the hypothesis of unity in the subject, to the exclusion of unity in the object, is consistent only, in Plato's opinion, with subjective idealism.

3. *The third Form of the Hypothesis.*

According to the third form of the sensual hypothesis, truth is a certain relation between sensations and their signs. Of all signs, the most extensive class is words. The relation between words and simple sensations was originally, in Plato's opinion, onomatopœic,[19] although the fact is now considerably disguised by the changes of time. He also considered that language was, in the first instance, formed by believers in the sensual theory.[20] But these admissions do not avail the defenders of that view, since the process of nomenclature implies that the unification of sensations is already completed; and this the hypothesis is, in Plato's opinion, unable to explain.

The same difficulty, in still greater force, besets the sensual view of the relation between the complex sensation and its complex sign. In proportion to the complexity both of the sign and of the significate, the greater is the number of unifications which must be accounted for.

Of the origin of the complex sensation, Plato discusses two possible theories. The first is, that the original elements generate a new product, possessing qualities which differ in kind from those of their elements, individually and collectively. The second is, that the original elements coexist unaltered in the result. The latter is his own opinion, the full significance of which will be better seen anon."

But, on either supposition, the same objection holds. In the former case, the new unification must be explained; in the latter, the old. In short, to the pretensions of nomenclature, in all forms from the logical definition by genus and difference, down to the unscientific descriptions of common sense, Plato opposes the same dilemma:—Either there is, or there is not, unity in the original sensation. If there be unity in the significate, unity need not be sought in the sign; and unless there be unity in the significate, it cannot be found in the sign.

And that, for the following reasons:—The process of nomenclature depends upon—first, the impression which the sensation leaves upon the issuer of the word; and, second, upon the particular sound which, he thinks, represents the impression. But as, upon the principles of sensualism, all impressions are equally impressions, every one's descriptions of everything are equally true. The process of nomenclature, then, not only not removes the original difficulty, but actually doubles it; since the issue of the word involves a new sensuous impression."

Plato examines three species of complex description. The first is ordinary unscientific observation, which depends wholly upon the casual impressions of the observer." The second is enumeration of details, which are practically endless, since the process is relative to the knowledge and purpose of the enumerator, and has no validity beyond the special case." The third is the logical definition by Genus and Difference. All three, in Plato's opinion, as explanations of truth, labour under the same vice. They double all the difficulties raised by the two preceding theories, without in the slightest degree contributing to their solution."

The three varieties of description are noticed now, principally, because they illustrate Plato's universal mode of thought. The one extreme is unscientific description, the result of undisciplined subjective feeling; the other is logical definition, the acme of scientific subjective consistency; midway stands ordinary enumeration of details, resembling the former in its specialty, and the latter in its more or less conscious efforts at precision." The third presupposes the first; and the second presupposes both the first and third; but the converse does not hold in either case. The first is, therefore, prior to the third, and both to the second, in the order of thought. The order of thought plays, as we shall see, an all-important part in the philosophy of Plato.

Logical definition, therefore, as the acme of subjective consistency, insures clearness, and prevents merely verbal disputes; but, as an index of objective truth, cannot stand higher than the sensuous impression of which it is the abstract. But, if truth be something more than the description of the whole of the complex sensation, it follows that truth is more than the description of a part of the same sensation. Plato, therefore, must have rejected nominalism as an exposition of the highest certainty.

But this conclusion must be carefully distinguished from the question, Was Plato Nominalist, Conceptualist, or Realist? To prevent complication, the question at issue between Plato and the sensual school will be waived for the instant, and the unification of sensations will be assumed to be completed.

Each of the above celebrated theories has two aspects—the one, subjective or psychological; the other, objective or metaphysical. In the former shape, they deal with mental states as subjective facts exclusively, without taking any cognizance of their value as objective witnesses; in the latter, they profess to throw light upon objective reality. Bearing this distinction in mind, it can, it is conceived, be easily shown that Plato held that nominalism was a portion of the correct theory of Subjective Logic.

Plato, with M. Comte, and Mr. Mill, holds that there is a Logic of Images, as well as a Logic of Signs. Every logical process has its internal counterpart." The object-matter of this logic, as it is conceived by Plato, is propositions mental as well as verbal. Of these, the mental proposition is prior, in the Order of Thought, to its verbal duplicate; but, as the parts of the latter are familiar to the student of logic, the verbal proposition will, for convenience' sake, be considered as the type of the logical process.

The verbal proposition consists of two extremes, the subject and the predicate; and the sign of their correlation is the copula. In the order of thought, the predicate presupposes the subject, but the converse does not hold; the copula presupposes both, but not *vice versâ*. The primary affection of propositions is the relation between the subject and its predicate. There is also, in Plato's opinion, a secondary affection of propositions—their truth or falsity; but the secondary affection need not be considered now.

The mental proposition is a sensuous picture, of which the subject is the principal figure; around this are grouped the accessories, which correspond to the verbal predicate; and the mode of posing them represents the copula. Between the parts of the mental picture, the same keeping prevails as in the verbal fac-simile. The order of thought arranges the two groups. A proposition, therefore, as Plato conceived it, whether mental or verbal, is the mutual relation between subject and predicate in relation to reality.[38]

But reality is twofold, subjective and objective; the latter, however, need not be considered here. The mental picture, when presented by the mind itself, is the subjective Platonic Opinion; and the same picture, presented through the percipient organs, is the Platonic Sensation. All sensuous states of mind are therefore, in Plato's psychology, pictures more or less complete, with a more or less conscious reference to fact.[39]

Now, in Plato's mode of thought, the sensuous picture possessed a larger *quantum* of reality than its verbal description:[40] any fragment of the picture was further removed from reality than the original in its perfect condition. *A fortiori*, the description of the fragment was still further removed from reality than the fragment itself. As to the value of abstract words, Plato therefore agreed with the nominalist.

Further, a general term is, in reality, an abbreviation of two propositions:—The first asserts that a fragment has been detached from the perfect image, the complex whole; the second asserts that the fragment has many duplicates, in different places, which are otherwise exactly alike. They are, accordingly, differenced in space only. To borrow a term from controversy, sensation is pluripresent. But space, in Plato's opinion, not only falls short of the vivacity of a sensuous impression, but is in reality a figment compounded of negative abstractions and of time, which is itself an abstraction, but of a positive kind. General terms denote, therefore, fragments of sensation, relatively to space. It follows that general terms, according to Plato, are less real than abstract terms, and therefore less real than a fragment of a sensuous state, and, *a fortiori*, less real than the complete state. For these reasons, it appears that Plato must have have been a nominalist.

The same result follows from a review of Plato's psychology. Sensations are conveyed to the mind through the various organs; sensations are also depicted in the imagination. To both of these are attached their verbal signs; but there is nothing more concrete than impressions, and there is nothing more abstract than signs. Between the sensation and sign there is nothing but a relation, perhaps originally onomatopœic, but essentially arbitrary. Plato, therefore, was not a conceptualist. He was, at least on the subjective side, a nominalist, as opposed to a conceptualist. His realism is not yet ripe for discussion.

But, to return to the point at issue between Plato and the sensual school: the subjective side of nominalism casts no light on the question in dispute—the unification of sensations. Not being able to find unity in the verbal sign, we are forced back upon the relation between sensations, and thence upon the sensation itself, and thus are finally landed in the first form of the sensual hypothesis. It is obvious, therefore, that nominalism does not solve the problem of philosophy as Plato conceived it. It is also plain that its products, abstract and general words, presuppose the notion unity, which they profess to supersede. The copy implies the original: the masterpieces of Zeuxis counterfeit the life; and the Iliad itself is but the shadow of a mighty age of heroes and of gods.[41]

4. *Negative Result:—Negative Logic.*

The general argument which Plato directs against every form of the sensual hypothesis may be summed up in an alternative:—If there be unity in the sensation, the hypothesis is not true; and if the hypothesis be true, there is no unity in the sensation. The result is altogether negative; and the conclusion is an example of the many discussions which in Plato lead to no positive result.

Negative logic was held by Plato to be the sole specific against the conceit of false knowledge."[2] If we are possessed by false opinions, the first proceeding must be to cast them out, and in this way prepare us to receive the true. But even though the negative process can substitute nothing in place of the conceit which it dispels, yet it is not altogether without fruit. We are at least thereby taught our ignorance, and rendered less disagreeable to others."[3] But the uses of negative logic do not stop here. Negative logic is not only a specific which acts directly on the disease, but also a tonic which gives the patient a relish for stronger food. So far negative logic verges on the positive. Its use in this latter respect is a corollary from Plato's view of the nature of a proposition.

Every proposition was, as we have seen, in his opinion, the relation of a predicate to its subject, with a further reference to reality. For example, the assertion, "Socrates drank hemlock," is a genuine proposition. The subject suggests its immortal prototype, and the predicate recalls the last sunset which he saw. It is also true. Echecrates believed that, if he had been with Phædo in the cell, he also would have seen Socrates drink the poison. On the other hand, if Echecrates stated to Phædo that Socrates had escaped from prison, the assertion would have been equally a genuine proposition, fully furnished with subject and predicate; but it would not have been true. Phædo, as soon as he understood the meaning of the terms, would have at once opposed his recollection of what actually occurred to the assertion of Echecrates. Both assertions were equally assertions—each had its subject, and each had its predicate. Each proposition called up a mental picture, containing no intrinsic impossibility. So far, the two assertions are on a par; but on reference to reality, they at once diverge. Between reality and the former assertion there is conformity, and between reality and the latter there is discrepancy; but no familiarity with what actually occurred in the prison would have enabled Phædo to contrast the proposition, Socrates drank hemlock, with such a skeleton as O. o. O. Two terms are required in every relation; and truth and falsity were, in Plato's opinion, relations between propositions and reality. To deny, is to assert that the relation truth does not exist between a proposition and reality. The two terms, reality and a proposition, are therefore indispensable.

The object of negative logic, as Plato conceived it, was therefore, not to make the mind a *tabula rasa*, but to connect a proposition indirectly with reality through the medium of another proposition. For example, in the case of the sensual hypothesis, the notion of permanent unity was familiar to every Greek who had dipped into the Eleatic philosophy; and the notion of a perpetual flux was widely disseminated by the disciples of Heracleitus. Plato, accordingly, by showing that flux was non-unity, and that unity was non-flux, in the first place, rendered each concept more clear; and, in the second, indirectly reminded his hearers that both propositions, taken in their thoroughgoing extent, could not at the same time have the same reference to reality. The terms unity and flux would at once have suggested to his hearers the universality which Parmenides and Heracleitus claimed for their respective doctrines. Through the medium of these implied majors the audience, by the aid of Plato's minors, drew the conclusion that the doctrines of the two schools could not both be sound. Plato's hearers were accordingly compelled either to reconcile the apparent antagonisms, or definitely to abandon either; but to abandon both was, in his opinion, impossible. The two notions being once given in their primary relation, as subject and predicate, their secondary relation truth or falsity, is an inevitable alternative; since it must be either true or false that sensation and unity, in their thoroughgoing extent, are incompatible. And, in the last place, Plato's example in some measure tended to produce in his hearers the elenchtic frame of mind. In these respects, negative discussion, in Bacon's phrase, directly bore light, and indirectly bore fruit.

Such were, in the view of Plato, some of the uses of negative logic; its higher functions can only be seen from the standing point of the Platonic ethics.

III.

SUPERSENSUOUS ENTITIES.

τίς ἀχὼ
Οὐδόντον, ἢ βρότειος, ἢ κεκραμένη ;
Prom. V. 115, *sq.*

EVERY organ of sensation is idiopathic; the presentation through each sense is in its ultimate phase unique. But in the background of the presentation we find certain entities, attached either to all sensations, or to some two or more.[1] Upon examination, these entities appear to have nothing in common with the idiopathic affection of the organ. The entities which Plato professes to discover have nothing to do with the finer links which observation discovers between the more obtrusive phenomena of the senses. The point on which he dwells does not clash with the results of modern experiment. Bacon's *dictum*, that experiment must judge the phenomenon, while observation registers the result of the experiment, deals with a matter entirely different. The Baconian precept, however invaluable as a means of unravelling the tangled skein of empirical sequences, does not touch the entities in question. Complex sensations can only be correlated with other sensations; and even were a single formula elicited which should sum the prerequisites of all presentations, still the presentation itself—the last link of the chain—would remain *sui generis*.¹ And it is precisely in the ultimate phase of sensation that the difficulty is found with which the Platonic philosophy professes to grapple.

Socrates, in the Phædo, relates his philosophical experiences; whether that account be historical or not, is quite immaterial. Its philosophical purport is confirmed by similar passages in other dialogues, and pre-eminently by the entire body of Platonic doctrine. It is, at all events, a statement of Plato's own reasons for renouncing the sensual belief. Sensualism is deliberately rejected, because the Heracleitan notion of indefinite flux cannot explain the facts of the percipient process, as Plato conceived it.

According to Heracleitus, all modes of being were modes of flux. Alterations in bulk and pattern were the only possible kinds of change. If, then, bulk and pattern remain unaltered, there is no alteration. On the principles of the Heracleitan system, the perception of change is impossible, since, *ex hypothesi*, change there was none. But Plato urges that every sensible object, its bulk and pattern remaining unaltered, may represent indifferently an equal, greater, or less degree of any and all of its sensible qualities, when compared with another specimen of the same kind.² Further, that the most opposite sensible facts may produce identical results, and identical sensible facts the most opposite results, bulk and pattern remaining totally unaltered. But, if identical sensible facts produce the most opposite results, and the most opposite sensible facts produce identical results, the influence of sensible facts is entirely eliminated. There is, accordingly, a residual fact which the Heracleitan doctrine cannot explain; the doctrine is not thoroughgoing, and therefore breaks down.

For example, a finger is not the less a finger because it differs from other fingers in size, colour, &c. The most marked differences in these qualities relatively to other fingers leave it a finger still. The whole presentation finger is given to the sight as a finger, and nothing more. But the degrees of Quantity and Quality which the finger possesses are, relatively to those of other fingers, capable of being construed, with regard to the quality selected for comparison, as equal, greater, or less.

Briefly, all sensible qualities are relative. But the Heracleitan doctrine only covers absolute change. The relativity of sensations, therefore, proves the doctrine false.

According to Plato, the object which is presented through the senses as actually one, is by some other faculty construed as possibly not one; that is, as capable of occupying different and opposite positions in the scale of comparison.' Every sensible quality is thus the subject of several predicates, which denote incompatible positions. The difficulty is not due to any imperfection of language, but is an inherent and inevitable characteristic of human thought.' Every sensible presentation, when made the subject of metrical comparison, is *in posse* equal, greater, or less of the kind at the same time, although the sensible presentation is actually one. The incompatible predicates are strictly limited to three, viz., equal, greater, and less of the kind or quality, and no other predicate is possible. There are, in consequence, two conclusions open to us, one of which we must choose, if we wish to preserve any logical coherence. The sensuous quality, or sum of qualities, either is or is not the entire object. If the sensuous quality be the entire object, then sense contradicts itself; for its three deliverances are at the same time equipotent and incompatible. If the sensuous quality or sum of qualities be not the entire object, there is something supersensuous which may clear up the difficulty. In the former case the result is nihilism, since the object has undergone no intrinsic or extrinsic change, and consequently preserves its sensuous *statu quo*, and yet is the subject of three incompatibilities. In the latter case, the deliverances of sense may be admitted, *quantum valeant*, for the wants of every-day life, and the purposes of physical science, while the antinomy is reserved for the consideration of a supersensuous faculty. The alternative, therefore, is to accept sensualism in its entirety of contradiction, or to posit the supersensuous. The latter course is, in Plato's opinion, the only refuge from nihilism.

A nearer approach to the supersensuous background of perception discovers no absolutely determined entity. The supersensuous background is a tendency either to a Mean between two Extremes, or to either of them indifferently. The state of indifference continues until a line be drawn which divides the *ci-devant* indifference into two incompatible but homogeneous subdivisions—the more or less of the quality in question. The two subdivisions are remitted to the state of indifference, as soon as the line of demarcation is withdrawn. In other words, no definite degree of any quantity or quality can be predicated, until some specimen or sample be selected from the entire scale of degrees in question, and set up as the standard of reference. The selection of a standard at one stroke divides the scale into two categories—the more or less of the quality under consideration. The fact that most nations have a fixed standard of the more practically important sensations, weight and extension, helps to conceal from ordinary attention the metaphysical significance of the percipient process; and in the case of the other sensations, such as colour and smell, where there is no recognised scale, an average sample is unconsciously made the mental basis of reference. But in either case the difficulty is merely shifted to the standard which law, usage, or caprice may have have selected.[*]

Every standard or index must be at the same time of its kind, and beyond its kind. Unless it is

to some extent of its kind, the kind can bear to it
no relation save diversity; and unless it is supposed
to be beyond its kind, its *quondam* fellows cannot
be referred to its adjudications. The notion of
every standard, therefore, involves as its constituents
partial similarity, and temporary absoluteness. Its
qualities, *quâ* absolute, cannot be called in question—
"Quis custodiet custodes?"

Some one degree, as has been observed, serves
ordinarily as the index of the scale; and the selection of an index removes all practical difficulties.
But the speculative question recurs, Whence comes
the provisional rank of the standard? The degrees of quantity and quality which make up the
scale receive their various limitations from the provisional standard; but the standard itself is, in
reality, a member of the scale. From what, then,
is the specific degree of the standard derived?
Not from the standard itself. Were it so derived,
the standard would be both absolute and relative
at the instant when the whole class, standard included, has no limitation whatsoever. Consequently
the whole class, standard included, is graduated by
something which is extern to the whole class,
standard included. The provisional standard, therefore, receives its limitation from some real standard.
The real standard, consequently, must be something
which exists over and above the indefinite possibility
of relation, as well as something over and above the
sum of actual relations which, including the stan-

dard, compose the scale. But, as this reasoning
applies to all relations of quantity and quality, it
follows that the relations or degrees of quantity and
quality constitute the residual fact, for which the
sensual hypothesis does not, in Plato's opinion, account. This is equivalent to saying that the degrees of quantity and quality have a supersensuous
basis.[1]

The actual relations or degrees of quantity and
quality may be denoted by the term Limitation;
and the indefinite possibility of relation, by the term
Receptivity. These terms will be, accordingly,
sometimes employed, for brevity's sake, throughout
the remainder of the section, but always in the
same sense.

All modes of Limitation contain two constituents.
Of these, the one is the bare, undetermined Receptivity; the other is the Point of Reference, extern to
the Receptivity, which reduces its indefinite possibility to definite actuality. And this complex notion,
containing the two constituents, is the first aspect
of the Idea.

The Idea is, consequently, first presented to us as
a supersensuous entity, which is the basis of all
scales of Limitation, as well as something more than
all the actual degrees which compose the scale or
kind. In Platonic language, the Idea is both The One
and The Many. In other words, the Idea contains
an element which is unique, and an element which
is indefinite. The Idea contains an element which

is unique, because it involves a single point of reference. The Idea likewise contains an element which is indefinite, because it involves an undetermined Receptivity. But undetermined Receptivity —that which is aloof from every relation—is the antithesis of The One, the acme of limitation. Receptivity is, therefore, The *non*-One ; and The *non*-One, construed in positive terms, is The Many.[9]

Between The One *per se* and Receptivity *per se* there is no relation save antithesis. But Receptivity, considered relatively to The One, admits the degrees of quality which, in the language of quantity, are equal, greater, and less. Now, the comparative notions greater and less may be denoted by the positive terms great and small; and we know from Aristotle,[10] that The Great and The Small were the technical terms used by Plato in his lectures, to signify Receptivity, apart from and out of all numerical relation, although the words great and small have a quantitative connotation. But a reference to something was unavoidable, since Receptivity *per se* is devoid of all attributes whatsoever. And as, in Plato's opinion, the terms of quantity have, of all words, the faintest tinge of sensuous colouring, terms of quantity are best fitted, or rather least unfitted, to describe the modes of supersensuous existence.[11]

The Idea is, we have seen, a combination of The One with The Indefinite—of Limitation with Receptivity. In and by that combination The Indefinite is limited by The One. The result of that limitation is a product which, as it holds the two elements in combination, takes, according to Plato, substantive rank as a *third* entity. Again, to recur to Plato's universal mode of thought, The Indefinite presupposes The One, but the converse does not hold; and the combination presupposes both, but the converse does not hold. . The One is, therefore, prior in the order of thought to The Indefinite; and both elements are prior in the same order to their combination the Idea. The significance of the order of thought will be seen anon.

In the mean time, the Idea may be described as Receptivity receiving its modes of Limitation from The One; or, conversely, as The One imposing on Receptivity its modes of Limitation:[13] the result is the threefold limitation, equal, greater, and less. But, as this threefold limitation covers all assignable degrees of quantity and quality in all sensible objects,[13] it follows that the Idea is the basis of all metrical scales, or kinds of quantity and quality in sensible presentations. In other words, the Idea is that which renders every sensation definite, and without which the sensation would be indefinite; that is, incogitable. Briefly, the Idea is the principle of definiteness, which, for the reasons given above, is held by Plato to be supersensuous.

Further, as sensation must be *some* colour, *some* sound, &c., Definiteness is the *sine quâ non* of sensation.[14] The sensible, therefore, presupposes the supersensuous, but the converse does not hold. The supersensuous is, consequently, prior in the order of thought.

From this discussion two positive results may be educed. The first is, that there is something supersensuous; the second is, that the supersensuous is the logical basis of the sensible. Whether that supersensuous basis be subjective, or objective, or both, remains to be seen. But, until this point be decided, it would be premature to attempt to translate Plato's view of quantity and quality into modern equivalents.

IV.

OBJECTIVE ENTITIES.

ὧν Ὄλυμπος
Πατὴρ μόνος, οὐδέ νιν
Θνατὰ φύσις ἀνέρων
Ἔτικτεν.—ŒD. R., 867, *sq.*

The Idea, up to this, appears only as the quantitative framework of the sensible presentation. The object-matter of perception, consequently, may be resolved into two elements—the sensible and the supersensuous. The two elements are distinct in the order of thought, but they are not co-ordinate; and the same reasons which establish their distinctness will likewise show why they are not co-ordinate.

The sensible and the supersensuous are diametrically opposite in character, and are best described by a series of contrary predicates. The objects of sense are not patent to the supersensuous faculty, while to sense all supersensuous objects are an unmeaning blank. The most general aspect of the sensible scheme is the law of causation, as understood by Hume and Brown—the *fact* of invariable antecedence and consequence, exclusive of all causal *nexus*. In the train of sequents, the consequent is

in immediate relation to its antecedent. But the
law of causation in either of its modes, antecedence
or consequence, growth or decay, does not bind the
supersensuous sphere.

For the following reasons:—Sensible impressions
are presented to the mind through the medium of
the several organs. That is, the organ is one among
other antecedents to sensation. Thus the eye is an
antecedent to the ultimate perception, colour. But,
according to Plato, the principle of Limitation has no
special medium. Limitation is found in the products of every organ, but differs totally from all of
them in character. Further, Plato held that there
is no *general* existence. For example, an eye sees
colour; but every colour must be particular; that
is, green, blue, &c. When, then, there is no special
organ—no medium with a special fitness—there is
no organ at all. Even if, as we must, we hold the
brain to be the ultimate organ of sensation, yet the
cerebral modification must take final shape as the
special antecedent to some special sensation. The
ultimate modification of the brain, if followed by
anything, must be followed by some particular degree of colour, sound, smell, &c. There is no abstract
sensation;[1] and it is precisely in the final consequence to cerebral antecedence, that Plato saw the
difficulty on which his system rests. The Idea, therefore, has no special organ.

But, if the idea be not presented through the medium of any organ, the Idea must be in immediate

connexion with its correlative faculty. The Idea, therefore, is properly an object of intuition. The Idea is an object of intuition; that is, the Idea has no antecedent: and where there is no antecedent, there can be no consequent. The Idea, in this way, is not subject to the law of antecedence and consequence. And, since time in Platonic language signifies a *portion* only of the fact of sequence,[1] it follows that time and its modes do not apply to the Idea. If, then, time does not apply to the Idea, the Idea is non-temporal. In positive language, therefore, the Idea is eternal.

Further, as the Idea is non-temporal, it is not subject to the law of sequence: as the Idea is not a temporal consequent, it cannot be dependent on any temporal antecedent. The Idea, accordingly, in positive terms, is self-sustained. It therefore exhibits a glaring contrast to every member of a sequence, as every member of a sequence is intimately connected with its immediate antecedent and consequent.

We may now see the meaning of the Platonic law of cognition—Like is known by Like. Like is known by like, because the percipient organ, like the perceived object, is a portion of a sequence; they are both antecedent elements, into which analysis resolves the ultimate resultant. Sensation, the organ, and the object, lie *in pari materiâ*. But, as was said, the Idea is not subject to the law of causation. It has, consequently, no antecedent which acts as a medium between it and its faculty; and, since immediacy regards alike the faculty and the object, the faculty is immediately related to the Idea. The faculty, therefore, is not subject to the law of sequence. But, as all objects of knowledge must be known, either mediately or immediately, and as the Idea has no mediating organ, the Idea must be an immediate object of its faculty. Consequently, the faculty and the object, being immediately related, are severally non-temporal: Like is known by Like. We shall also see that the faculty and the Idea together do not constitute a sequence.

The Platonic law of cognition is not a hypothesis which Plato assumes, in order to explain or account for the *fact* of knowledge. The law is an abstract of psychological observations. The principle, like is known by like, means, when expanded, that like is known *as* like, as well as by like.[3] The law is put in evidence, not to prove the fact of knowledge, but to express concisely the character of that fact. In the case of sensible perception, the organ and object are known as similar. In the case of noetic intuition, objects are known by a faculty which, in the cognitive process, *eo ipso* apprehends itself, as well as its object, and in consequence of such apprehension predicates mutual similarity. In the process of self-apprehension the higher cognitive faculty sees that it is nothing but itself, and consequently distinguishes itself from the law of antecedence and consequence. That is, to say, immediate knowledge—

intuition—knows that it is not mediate knowledge—sensation. But, as all knowledge must be either immediate or mediate, intuition and sensation are the two poles of the sphere of cognition. Hence, the formula which sums the process of intuition and of sensation expresses the possible forms of all cognition, and such a formula is the Platonic law of knowledge—Like is known by Like.

Plato, then, was amply justified in positing two classes of mental objects—the noetic objects of intuition, and the sensible objects of mediate perception. The noetic entity is not a partial affection of the bodily organ—the sensation is; the Idea is not logically dependent—the sensation is; the Idea is not subject to sequence—the sensation is. The Idea is an eternal object of intuition, while the sensation is a transient impression. The Idea and the sensation are, consequently, diametrically contrasted; there cannot be a better marked antithesis.

Of the *locale* of the Idea there can be but three theories. The Idea must exist in a state which either does, or does not, derive its existence from the human percipient. The Idea, therefore, must be either wholly subjective, wholly objective, or partly both. The last hypothesis may be summarily rejected. To make the Idea a resultant analogous to sensation, would stultify the entire purport of Plato's teaching; the unchangeable cannot change. On the first hypothesis, the cognitive subject and its object, the Idea, are but different names for the same thing.

OBJECTIVE ENTITIES.   49

The object, the Idea, being the workmanship of the mind, is in reality a mental phase. On the objective hypothesis, the Idea enjoys a substantive individuality, apart from the human mind. The objective hypothesis is the view of Plato.

For these reasons, among others:—The Idea is the Principle and Law of Quantity and Quality. No portion of the sensible universe can be construed to intelligence, save as actually quantified and qualified. Every portion has its kind and its degree. If, then, the Idea—the Principle and Law of Quantity and Quality'—be a subjective modification of the percipient subject, the main constituent of the universe the Idea, is a subjective concept; and in the absence of the numerical or quantifying principle, The Other Element was, in Plato's opinion, incogitable. It is Indefinite. The universe—the combination of Quantity and The Indefinite—is, therefore, directly and indirectly a concept whose existence is commensurate with the duration of the act and process of subjective thinking. The universe is directly a subjective concept, because the Idea is a mode of the human mind. It is indirectly a concept, because The Other Element, the Indefinite, depends upon the Idea as its logical *sine qua non*. Consequently, the universe is directly and indirectly a phase of human thought. But such a conclusion contradicts consciousness, as set forth in the law of cognition. Consciousness apprehends the object as distinct from the subject; that is to say, as something more than the process

of thinking.[*] On the other hand, if the universe be
regarded as a mental state, which is partly above
and partly below the horizon of consciousness—as a
mode of the human mind, in part patent, and in part
latent—the hypothesis contradicts itself. Thought
exists in thinking only; slightly to alter Berkeley's
formula, its *esse* is *concipi*. When self-consciousness
is absent, thought is in abeyance; thought cannot
be thinking and not-thinking. The universe, consequently, *qua* not-thought, is non-existent; and the
second variety of subjective idealism is reducible to
the first, and in that shape is confronted by intuition. The universe is, therefore, not a mere mode of
human thought, either wholly or partially patent to
consciousness.[*] It is not a disk which owes its phases
to the reflection of the subject. Consequently, in
Plato's opinion, the Idea possesses a substantive individuality, utterly independent of the human mind.
The consideration of The Other Element just now
would be premature.

The most generally received hypothesis is, that all
mental objects are products generated by the reci-
procity of subject and object; that all knowledge involves, of necessity, a mutual alteration in and by
both subject and object. Now, this conception of
knowledge diverges most widely from Plato's line
of thought. Plato, certainly, held that sensation is
a product of the heteropathic kind. Sensation pure
and simple cannot, in his opinion, be resolved into
its components; and the division of the sum into

OBJECTIVE ENTITIES. 51

organ and object is strictly relative to the mind in a second and distinct state of sensation. It is, consequently, open to an objector to ask—May not intuition be a process strictly analogous to sensation? Granting, for argument's sake, the existence of the higher faculty intuition, may not its results be the product of factors whose several powers are indistinguishable? But Plato will not allow the word sensation to include anything more than the sum of separate concrete facts which it actually covers. Sensation, according to him, is the correlation of an organ of sense with its sensible object. Both terms must relate to the concrete particulars, vision, smell, touch, taste, hearing, or as many more of the same class as further research may disclose. It is obvious, however, that physiological research can only swell the number of the antecedents to the final perception. Sensation, therefore, can only mean, that where there is an antecedent, the law of antecedence and consequence is of necessity attracted. It also follows, that where there is no organ, there is no mediacy; that is to say, no antecedence, and so no consequence. But here intuition pronounces its final judgment; intuition is immediate knowledge, and immediate knowledge cannot be bound by the law or fact of antecedence and consequence. Each word has its own significate, but beyond that its dominion expires: if there be mediate knowledge, there must be immediate knowledge somewhere. To extend, then, the analogy of mediate knowledge to all knowledge is in itself preposterous, and in its results is confronted by intuition. The analogy of sensible sequence cannot, therefore, in Plato's opinion, be without absurdity extended beyond its special sphere. It cannot, consequently, be employed to deprive the Idea of its objective substantiality.

Of all Plato's conceptions, the objective substantiality of the Idea is most alien to the spirit of modern thought. It seems just as if a child were to imagine that the scale of a barometer caused, as well as helped to register, the weather. Number, as modern Empiricism conceives it, is the highest and most general abstraction: but the highest abstraction is also the least real; it holds the smallest possible quantity of contents; it is the smallest chipping of the solid block. Further, it is alleged, the mystery which, in Plato's opinion, requires the interposition of the Idea, may be fully laid bare by the laws of association. There is nothing in nature unique—its book contains no ἅπαξ λεγόμενον. Each degree of every sensible quality has innumerable fellows, more or less like, as well as more or less different. Accordingly, what is called the positive degree of any quality *suggests* the two comparative degrees. It is also true as a psychological fact, that all sensations are relative, not only, of course, to the percipient faculty, but also as between themselves. The process of abstraction, the laws of association, and the fact of the relativity of psychological phenomena are, it is alleged, potent enough to exorcise the Platonic Idea, and to doom it to the region of chimæra.

This view is so very prevalent, that the other side will scarcely obtain a provisional hearing. But the Writer ventures to think, that the objectivity of the Idea is the corner-stone of Platonism. Its value as a contribution to philosophy is quite another question, which must not, however, be prejudged. The objectivity of the Idea has its source in the Heracleitan doctrine of indefinite flux. That conception expressed, we saw, the modern notion of causation—an antecedent passes into its consequent through a stage of indifference. Be all ultimate physical composition either mechanical or chemical (subject, however, to psychological analysis), Plato's conception of the mutual relation of phenomena remains unshaken. But what he denied was, that the law of antecedence and consequence could be extracted from the Heracleitan doctrine of flux. Flux, according to Heracleitus, was thoroughgoing; everything was flux, and there was nothing which was not flux. But the same analysis which resolves the immediate phenomenon into Antecedent, Consequent, and Indifference, may, as was shown, disengage from each sequent three similar constituents, and so on to infinity. Unity, therefore, said Plato, cannot be found in the recession to infinity; since flux accompanies the recession, and unity is not flux. But the very notion of an immediate phenomenon involves unity somewhere;

Unity must be in either the subject *per se*, or in the object *per se;* for the third possibility—that unity lies in the junction of subject and object—is really the Heracleitan doctrine. In other words, the Heracleitan and Platonic hypotheses take sides as opposed possibilities. But, if there be unity in either the subject or in the object, the Heracleitan doctrine is not thoroughgoing, and is therefore not true; the sensual hypothesis is, accordingly, put out of consideration. The question is thus narrowed to the issue between a unity which is subjective and nothing more, and an objective unity somewhere. But, for the reasons (among others) given above, Plato rejects subjective idealism; and as there is, in his opinion, no existence without a basis of unity, it follows that, if the Idea exist objectively, it must possess as a *sine quâ non* objective unity. The objective substantiality of the Idea is a recoil primarily from the Heracleitan doctrine, and secondarily from subjective idealism; but its full significance cannot be seen as yet. The Idea has only been presented to us as the supersensuous, as well as objective, Principle and Law of Limitation. But this view, though in Plato's opinion true, lies only on the surface.

V.

THE OBJECTIVE UNIVERSE.

'Ουρανόθεν δ' ἄρ ὑπερράγη ἄσπετος αἰθήρ.—Hom. *Il.* viii. 558.

As every form of the sensual hypothesis has proved unsatisfactory, supersensuous essence has of necessity been posited. We have also seen that supersensuous essence contains, in Plato's opinion, an objective element. The next step, consequently, is to determine the nature and form of the objective supersensuous world, as Plato conceived it.

The systems of philosophy current in Plato's day were all reducible to three ground forms. Of these the first was the scheme of Parmenides, the hypothesis of absolute unity—of unity which is unity and nothing else—of unity utterly aloof from all possible relation whatsoever. The direct antithesis of this scheme was the Heracleitan hypothesis of indefinite flux, which has been already noticed. Between these counter schemes Plato endeavoured to effect a compromise, the materials for which he found in the schools of Empedocles and Pythagoras.[1] Plato's scheme is, consequently, an amalgamation of the thoroughgoing Absoluteness of Parmenides and the thoroughgoing Relativity of Heracleitus. But, as in his opinion the Relative presupposes the Absolute, the Parmenidean scheme is prior in the order of thought to that of Heracleitus; and both schemes are, consequently, prior to his own.

The Heracleitan hypothesis of indefinite flux has been already examined. Thoroughgoing flux cannot, in Plato's opinion, account for the notion unity. But, if Heracleitus ignored unity, the same charge cannot certainly be brought against Parmenides.

The Parmenidean scheme is the position of Absolute unity—of unity utterly untrammelled by all possible relations; of unity limited only by, and completely by, itself; of unity changeless and self-sustained. The Parmenidean unity, consequently, cannot enter into either the more general relation existence, or into the more special relation knowledge. The scheme of unity cannot, therefore, account for the facts to which intuition testifies. The subject apprehends itself, and *eo ipso* apprehends the object— knowledge of what a thing is, according to Plato, is knowledge of what it is not. If, then, the scheme of thoroughgoing unity be accepted, all the facts of consciousness must be given up as phenomenal illusions. All differences, either in pure thought, or in emotive apprehension, must be abandoned as unreal. The existence of diversity, as exhibited by intuition, is in Plato's opinion fatal to the scheme of Parmenides.[3]

On the other hand, the notion unity cannot be totally abrogated. In the absence of substantial unity, phenomenal existence is a chaos of warring incompatibilities; and if we follow the negation of unity, into its consistent results, phenomenal existence is incogitable. Whatever, therefore, may be the attendant difficulties, unity must be posited as the basis of phenomenal diversity.*

The existence of diversity or relation as an object of noetic intuition is as fatal to the scheme of absoluteness, as the existence of unity is to the rival scheme of relativity. But, as everything must be either absolute or relative—that is to say, must exist completely in and by itself, or in and by connexion with some other thing—Plato's hypothesis remains as a last resource, perhaps things are *both* absolute and relative. Unity may exist on the one side, diverging towards absoluteness; and, on the other, converging to relation.

Plato, accordingly, with Parmenides, posits an objective unity, but allows it a capacity of sustaining divers relations, of which it is the logical and substantive basis; and thus emerges the Platonic scheme of objective diversities or *relations*, crystallizing round the central form, unity. Where there is relation, there must be a basis of that relation; but it does not of necessity follow that the sum of actual relations commeasures the ulterior residuum of possibility.* The scheme of Plato may be described as a system of diversities, or pluralities, dependent on unity, which is in all respects independent of relation, save so far as it is related to its dependents. The unity of Parmenides is

"A star, and dwells apart,"

in unbroken and eternal solitude; the unity of Plato is a central sun, begirt with hosts of kindred spheres.

In all schemes of diversity in company with unity, diverse entities may coexist in one of three shapes:— Diverse entities may coexist in complete distinctness; or in complete coincidence; or in partial distinctness, and, consequently, in partial coincidence. The hypothesis of complete distinctness may be at once rejected. It unites at once all the difficulties both of the position and of the negation of unity. Unity exists, but there is a vast gulf between it and all relation. The next hypothesis, complete coincidence, necessitates the fusion, and ultimately the identity, of all diversities; all diversity is swallowed up in the changeless blank of the Parmenidean One. The mixed hypothesis of partial distinctness and partial coincidence alone remains, which developes itself somewhat as follows:—

The Platonic law of cognition, we have seen, is, Like is known by Like. The psychic principle in its highest state sees by intuition that the supersensuous object is like itself; Like is cognised as Like, as well as by Like, since self-cognition is involved in the noetic faculty. Now, intuition discovers in the psychic principle the opposed states of what Plato calls Rest and Motion, and their compromise, or indifference. Rest and Motion denote, respectively, not merely local and temporal change, but also the elements of noetic diversity—the absolute and relative constituents of pure thought and emotive apprehension. Local and temporal alteration can only be conceived relatively to space and time; but these forms, as we shall see, do not penetrate the deeper strata in either subject or object. Rest and Motion in the noetic region denote, therefore, only notional difference in the order of thought, the differentiating law of higher existence.[a]

But thought, as Plato conceived it, is not a mere logical abstraction. Thought is a mode of the highest life—the indissoluble combination of intuition and of emotive tact. The psychic principle holds both elements in union, without either of them neutralizing the specific virtues of the other. Hence, then, noetic Rest and Motion denote the elements of all the higher states of the psychic principle. Rest is the absolute element; Rest denotes the rational and formative agent. Motion is the relative element: Motion denotes the emotional, undetermined spontaneity, which is to be formed by the other. The indifference or the combination of the two extremes—Rest and Motion, constitutes the higher psychic existence, which, as supersensuous, is not bound by the sensuous forms, time or space. Of these elements, the emotive presupposes the rational. The emotive movement is called into play by the presence of its object. The object of emotion is seen by the cognitive faculty, and without the cognitive faculty the object of emotion is *nil*. The combination of both elements presupposes each element *per se;* and thus the precedency of the psychic elements in the order of thought is Rest, Motion, Indifference.

But, since the order of thought is the single law which differentiates higher existence, and as Like is known by Like, Plato discovers similar elements in the objective world. The two laws—the law of the order of thought, and the law of cognition—are the keys of the Platonic ontology. If the two laws be kept steadily in view, and the binary constituents of noetic reality—cognitive and emotive power—be not forgotten, the remainder of the discussion will present no difficulty.

Corresponding sets of entities are, accordingly, found in both the subjective and the objective spheres: in each, noetic activity presupposes noetic quiescence. Each set of relations rests on an ulterior basis of unity—the Platonic *sine quâ non* of all existence, phenomenal or real. Now, Rest and Motion are complete contraries. Rest and Motion can only enter into combination through a stage of indifference—a state which partakes equally of both extremes. But the union of Rest and Motion in indifference is that combination of the absolute and the relative which constitutes the higher psychic existence. Both Rest and Motion coincide, therefore, with a *portion* of existence, the whole of which they do not severally commeasure. The higher existence is a wider entity than either Rest or Motion.

Every entity possesses, relatively to itself, identity. Every entity possesses, relatively to other entities, diversity. Hence, the two entities, or relations, identity and diversity, exercise an all-pervading but unequal influence in the noetic hierarchy. Rest and Motion possess, each its own, several identity. Rest and Motion, accordingly, bear to that portion of the higher existence with which they severally coincide the relation identity. On the other hand, Rest and Motion *inter se* are contraries; each presents to the other the relation diversity. But Rest and Motion do not either severally or jointly commeasure the whole of the higher noetic existence.⁶ In Plato's mode of thinking, the combination of two elements is a third moment in the noetic process. Rest and Motion, therefore, *quâ* elements, bear to existence, *quâ* combination, the relation diversity. Rest and Motion, consequently, as contrasted with their combination, are diverse to existence, and consequently distinct from existence. Rest and Motion, so far, therefore, are modes of non-Existence.

Existence, also, *quâ* combination, is diverse to its elements, Rest and Motion—actuality does not commeasure possibility. Consequently, existence, *quâ* combination, is not coextensive with the sum total of Being. Hence, then, Existence, *quâ* combination, belongs to non-Existence. Existence, in a certain relative sense, is non-existent.

The apparently strange term, *non*-Existence, does not signify zero. To the noetic faculty—intuition—non-Existence denotes a relative, but real entity. Relation, though subsequent to independent existence in the order of thought, is to the eye of reason no less real than the antecedent terms which compose its basis. But, as relation is a function of two or more variables, relation can never be in itself determinate. Like a light reflected from several luminous bodies, its full power is dependent on the respective contributions. Identity, on the other hand, shines by no borrowed lustre, but emanates from internal essence. Hence, identity occupies a more determinate position in the noetic sphere than relativity. Non-Existence, therefore, in Plato's language, signifies, not mere zero, but every relative mode of existence which presupposes an ulterior basis, logical as well as substantive.

All Existence, according to Plato, is grounded on an ulterior nucleus of unity. To this extent Existence and Unity coincide, and are so far identical. But Existence itself, so far as it is a combination of elements, is in Plato's mode of thinking distinct from its elements considered in themselves. Now, the category non-Existence signifies all modes of relative existence. The combination Existence, consequently, belongs to the category non-Existence;

since the notion of a combination is subsequent in the order of thought to the elements which compose it.

But Rest, Motion, and Existence, possess, each its own, identity; they are each distinct in character. Hence, Rest, Motion, and Existence are to some extent distinct from unity, the paramount entity. Rest, Motion, and Existence, therefore, belong to The not-One; but the term non-One, clothed with a positive dress, is The Many. We thus discover in the objective sphere the two constituents of the Idea, The One and The Many.

To dwell a little longer on the two entities, The One and The Many:—As all entities ultimately run up into unity, all entities partially coincide with unity. That is to say, all entities are in part identical with unity. On the other hand, all entities, so far as they do not coincide with unity, so far diverge from it, and are thus far distinct. So far as they are distinct from unity, they are opposed to unity, and in this shape constitute an indefinite aggregate, or what Coleridge calls Multiety. But even the term Multiety conveys too much, since it involves a faint reference to quantity. Plurality is still more inappropriate. In the absence of unity, a genuine plurality is impossible, since a plurality is an association of units. We thus discover in their purity, the two elements of noetic reality. The first is the limiting or unifying monad, the formative principle of the noetic sphere. The second is the indefinite, the unlimited, or ununified receptivity, the material element in the same region. The word material has no reference to the Matter of modern metaphysics.

These two elements—The One and The Indefinite—are not of co-ordinate importance. Receptivity, or The Indefinite, can only be conceived in some relation, upon which it ceases to be indefinite. In itself, The Indefinite is strictly incogitable. The Indefinite presupposes The One; but the converse does not hold. The One is, therefore, prior in the order of thought.

Let us now apply the explanation, given a little before, of the elements of the higher psychic life. As Rest is in the subject, so is The One in the object; and as Motion is in the subject, so is The Indefinite in the object. But Like is known by Like: the objective Indefinite is, therefore, undetermined spontaneity, aloof from all contact with intelligence.'

To continue: Unity and The Indefinite are in complete antithesis; but the chasm which separates them is bridged by an ethical apprehension. Unity, which intellect apprehends as the zenith of the cognitive hemisphere, is revealed to ethical feeling as subjected to super-essential and supreme Perfection. Unity is thus a position of the intellect, and Perfection an apprehension of the emotive element. But, as was said, Unity and supreme Perfection are not without their connecting link. Unity and Perfection blend in the notion Causal Efficiency.* The notion Cause answers the intellectual demand for a prime antecedent, and the notion Efficiency satisfies the emotive craving for objective personality; and the same notion—perfect causal efficiency—is at once the motive and the means to a union between The One and the Indefinite. Of these constituents, the objective sphere of Plato is composed.

The objective sphere, as Plato conceived it, is, in modern language, the Divine Personality, the rationale of whose proceedings is as follows:—At the instance of super-essential Perfection, supreme Intelligence evolves the quantifying mould which, in the hand of efficient Will, fashions the plastic Spontaneity of the Divine nature; and the product in its final shape is the Idea, viewed on its objective side.

The Idea, in modern language, is the completed act of the Deity, when He submits Himself to the relations which are determined by Supreme Intelligence, and effectuated by Supreme Will. The Idea is God in the act of manifestation.

In the supersensuous sphere, the order of thought is the only law. The world of thought is governed by the law of thought. In the order of thought, the Idea is the outer surface of the sphere. The full notion, of a perfect intelligent and autonomous Being entering into relation, necessitates the following precedency in its constituents, according to the order of thought:—*First*, before which there is nothing, the supreme and inscrutable substance, The Good.

Of The Good, according to Plato, our notion is but negative—we know that it must be, but cannot as yet know it as it is. *Second*, the supreme intelligence, which sees the sum total of possibilities. *Third*, the indefinite and undetermined spontaneity, not yet exerted in subordination to intelligence. And, *Fourth*, the specific act of volition, motived by Supreme Goodness, and guided by Supreme Intelligence. Strictly speaking, the third and fourth notions differ only as actuality is distinct from possibility; and the synthesis of the three is the Idea.

The constituents of the Idea require some special consideration. The basis of the structure is that entity which, as The Good, verges on the absolute, and, as The One, verges on the relative. The basis is, accordingly, conceived negatively as The Good, and positively as The One. Now, the antithesis of unity is The Indefinite; since unity is the very acme of limitation, and its contrary must be that entity which stands aloof from all limitation whatsoever; that is, The Indefinite. As, however, The Indefinite, standing apart from all limitation, is incogitable, The Indefinite is construed to thought as receptivity, the bare possibility of becoming a term in relation. But receptivity, being conceivable only in relation to limitation, is subsequent thereto in the order of thought. Receptivity presupposes limitation; the recipient of relation presupposes something which imposes it; but the converse does not hold. Further, both Unity and Receptivity are prior in the order of thought to their joint product, the Idea. The product presupposes its producers—the combination involves its elements; but the converse does not hold. The Idea, therefore—the joint product—the combination of Unity and The Indefinite—is subsequent to both Unity and The Indefinite in the order of thought.

We may now see the meaning of the Platonic Numbers. The last step of the noetic process—the completed Idea—presupposes: *first*, the combination of, *second*, the Indefinite; and of, *third*, The One. Each movement upwards brings us to a residue whose constituents decrease in number, but increase in noetic importance, and in substantive independence. Setting ourselves at the subjective centre of observation, the Idea is, I., the first definite step beyond the sensuous indefinite. But the Idea, as I., is the result; of II., the combination; of III., the Indefinite; and of IIII., Unity. Reversing the process, and standing at the objective centre, we see at a glance that the Idea contains *four* distinct noetic moments, or distinct steps in the order of thought. The Idea is a Result of a Combination of Two Elements, of which the former indirectly, and the latter directly, rests on an absolute Basis. The result presupposes the combination; the combination presupposes its two elements: of the two elements, the consequent presupposes the antecedent; but the antecedent is self-sustained. That is to say, The.

IIII. presupposes The III.; The III. presupposes The II.; The II. presupposes The I.; while The I. is self-sufficing, and verges on the absolute. But, since IIII. + III. + II. + I. = X., we may see how, in Plato's mind, The Ten denoted not only the highest form, but also the living substance of Supreme Reality. This is one of the many examples which show the absurdity of seeing in Plato merely a doctrine of abstract notions in an imaginative shape.

Further, we may also see from this the meaning of certain statements of Aristotle. According to Aristotle, Plato's Eidetic or Ideal Numbers could not enter into combination with each other. If we remember the Platonic law of the order of thought, the meaning of Aristotle's statement is at once apparent. That law was, that of two given entities one might presuppose the other, but that the converse did not of necessity hold. The latter clause has been perpetually overlooked, although it is of the very essence of the law. It draws a broad line between progressive notions, and notions which are strictly correlative. Of the latter, either of two indifferently at once suggests the other. For example, of correlatives, the notion up at once suggests the notion down, and the notion down at once suggests the notion up. Either may indifferently be made the starting point. But the case of what may be called progressive notions is very different. The latter notion presupposes the former; but the converse does not hold. For example—to take an illustration used for other purposes by M. Cousin and Mr. Mill—the notion effect is relative to the notion cause; that is, strictly, the notion effect presupposes the notion cause; but it does not follow that the cause is nothing but a cause. To take an illustration from Plato himself:—The soul is a principle, or beginning, as contrasted with certain consequent facts; but to suppose the soul to be nothing but a beginning would, as we shall see, stultify the entire teaching of Plato. Let us now apply the law of the order of thought to the noetic numbers.

In that order, The IIII. presupposes The III., but not conversely; The III. presupposes The II., but not conversely; The II. presupposes The I., but not conversely. Each of the four prime noetic numbers is, accordingly, differenced by its position in the noetic hierarchy. It can never change that position, since it is differenced as thought; and thought, as understood by Plato, is the life and substance of the noetic sphere. In other words, neither time nor space, however understood, binds noetic existence. Hence, then, each ascending noetic number describes, and not merely symbolizes, a less complex, but more substantial, state of spiritual life. Each rest in the ascent becomes broader, and more secure. In the process of abstraction, the case is exactly the reverse. The other uses of the Platonic numbers will be treated of as they arise; but it will, it is conceived, be evident that the Platonic number was neither a *quasi*-personification of the arithmetical concept, nor a misconception of the process of nomenclature. On the contrary, it must be repeated that the noetic or ideal number is the ground form of the Highest Spiritual essence, as Plato conceived it, and that too in the most strict and literal sense.

The constituents of the Idea require some still further consideration. The Idea is, we have seen, a result of the combination of two elements—The One and The Indefinite; but the term combination must not be allowed to lead us astray. According to Plato's mode of thought each element of a combination preserves in and during the combination its specific character. Consequently, in the Idea, The One remains The One, and is nothing but The One; and The Indefinite remains The Indefinite, and is nothing but The Indefinite. But, as The Indefinite, *quâ* The Indefinite, repudiates all modes of quantity whatsoever, The Indefinite, as such, cannot be construed as either whole or part. The notions whole and part are strictly modes of quantity. Hence, the Parmenides of the so-named dialogue reproves the youthful Socrates, for conceding Ideas to the higher concepts of ethics, and refusing them to such petty and disagreeable objects as mud and filth. What we, in our present condition, regard as loathsome and insignificant contains, according to Plato, the Idea in its binary dimensions as The One and The Indefinite. The One is there as The One, and The Indefinite is there as The Indefinite. The whole objective universe is nothing more than the Idea, and what we consider its meanest fragment is nothing less. But, as it is the glory of modern physics to conceive every thing as a mere question of fact, possibly patent to the senses, it follows, as has been already observed, that the greatest discoveries of modern physics do not touch Plato's peculiar views. The question at issue between Plato and the sensual school cannot be decided by experiment. The war in heaven may affect the earth; but the event cannot be altered by human aid. The contending hosts of earth-born giants and of gods must settle their quarrel, on their own ground, and with their own weapons.*

As all material relations are inapplicable to the noetic sphere, it follows that Ideas do not bear the same relation to the noetic universe which material parts bear to a material whole. To use a Platonic illustration, they are not as features to a face. Ideas are cognate acts of the same individuality, to which they are related somewhat as separate actions to the whole compass of personality. The Ideas result from the subjection of the non-intellectual personality to intellectual limitation. As a further consequence of such limitation, Ideas are severally unique, since they receive their respective positions from their constitutive law. Their constitutive law is the *quantum* of personality exerted, and the *quantum* of intelligence superimposed. Ideas are, therefore, individually distinct.

Ideas are also distinct in another respect—they are ultimate evolutions of the same personal *residuum*. In the order of thought, they are the joint consequents of One Prime Antecedent. They presuppose their antecedent, but their antecedent does not presuppose them. Ideas are, therefore, in the order of thought, distinct from their common antecedent. But the law of the order of thought differentiates the noetic sphere. The Idea, therefore, by the law of its being, is distinct from the paramount entity of the noetic hierarchy. We have also seen that it is likewise differenced from its co-ordinates. But the full significance of the Idea will not be apparent until the ethical views of Plato are placed in their proper pre-eminence.

Without wishing to anticipate the ethical questions, one thing may be stated here. The Idea, and, a *fortiori*, The Good, cannot be seen in their transparent clearness as long as our mental ken is obstructed by this mundane atmosphere. The Idea cannot even be adequately described. Speech is the reflex of human thought, and human thought is never wholly free from the intrusions of sense. Speech, consequently, never quite loses the stains of its sensuous origin, and in partially removing them nearly all its colour vanishes. The terms of quantity are most remote from the immediate objects of the senses; but they are, at the same time, the most bloodless and impersonal of abstractions. And thus the world of spirit, instinct with rich and varied life, must be drawn in colours which are only appropriate so far as they are faint, and abstract unity is the least illusive symbol of that Perfection, whose paler phase of Supreme Intelligence transmits the light of Justice and the glow of Beauty to the kindred Soul of Man."[16]

VI.

PARTICIPATION.

'Ως δ' ὅτε τοῖχον ἀνὴρ ἀράρῃ πυκινοῖσι λίθοισι
Δώματος ὑψηλοῖο, βίας ἀνέμων ἀλεείνων·
'Ως ἄραρον.

Hom. *Il.* xvi. 212, *sq.*

The analysis of a sensible object into its two elements, the noetic and the sensible, expresses, we have seen, the total contrariety of its constituents. But, as a faculty is only known in relation to its object, the contrariety of objects likewise expresses the contrariety of faculties.[1] Hence, the noetic faculty is blind to the peculiar matter of the senses, and the sensible faculty ignores noetic existence. Further, since the sensible object is composed of two elements only, the ascertainment of one leads of necessity to the ascertainment of the other.

We have also seen, that the Idea is the main constituent of the sensible presentation. Every sensible object admits explicitly one, and implicitly two predicates of quantity; the one explicitly denoting what is called the positive degree; and the two latter, the contrary comparatives—the more or the less of the thing in question. But this scale or framework of quantity was, in Plato's opinion, an object of the noetic faculty only, and as such was accordingly ignored by sense. If, therefore, we remove from the sensible presentation its intelligible scale of quantity, we must find, by way of residue, the specific matter, or, if the word will be allowed, the *peculium* of the senses.

The sensible element is not, in Plato's opinion, necessarily delusive. The deliverances of sense are not at all points at variance with the judgments of the higher faculty.[e] They are the necessary preliminaries to that higher knowledge for which Plato so strenuously contends. They answer the uses of every-day life. They also enable the observer of physical sequences to predict and to control the future. But the sensible element in perception is equivalent to a great deal more than this. The sensible element contains what is now generally divided into the primary and secondary qualities of matter, but between which Plato recognised no distinction. The sensible element constituted, in his opinion, the raw material of the lower pleasures and pains. It is also an object of belief, though not of knowledge in the higher sense of the term. For these reasons, it follows, that Plato did not regard the sensible *peculium* as either delusive or chimerical. He resisted, as we shall see, the claims of the senses to be the sole witnesses to the facts of consciousness; but he largely availed himself of their testimony, when they were confined to their proper sphere. In fact, the end of the Platonic philosophy was to relegate the senses to their due position.

The *peculium* of the senses was, in Plato's language, The Indefinite. It will be remembered that The Indefinite, as such, is incogitable. Consequently, the *peculium* of the senses, the sensible Indefinite, stripped of its noetic framework, is perfectly unknowable. But, viewed relatively to a framework of limitation, the sensible Indefinite presents the appearance of a train of antecedents and consequents. If then, we can ascertain, or at least approximate to ascertaining, the raw material out of which the series of antecedents and consequents is finally shaped, we have proportionately approximated to the sensible *residuum* of the percipient process.

The Idea, we have also seen, is a combination of two elements—Unity and The Indefinite. To use an arithmetical illustration, which Plato would scarcely have regarded as metaphorical, the Idea may be conceived as a fraction. The numerator will represent the noetic formula, the *quantum* of limiting intelligence; and the denominator will mark out, relatively to other Ideas, the *quantum* of personal energy or spontaneity, which is placed at the disposal of the special formula. In brief, the Idea contains two elements—the one rational, and the other emotive—understanding these words to connote objective reality.[*]

But the subject, the psychic principle, also contains two corresponding elements—intelligence and emotive energy. The Idea, consequently, by its double constitution, as intelligence, and personal activity, appeals to the cognate elements in the human subject. Human intelligence apprehends the quantifying formula, and human feeling responds to the contact of emotive personality. And so the subjective combination of intelligence and emotive energy apprehends the objective combination of intelligence and emotive energy—the mind reads off, or construes, the objective Indefinite in connexion with, and relatively to, its limiting formula—Like is known by Like.

The Idea is, therefore, the objective antecedent of perception; and the sensible Indefinite which is peculiar to each class of sensations is at least connected with the objective Indefinite allocated to each Idea. The matter peculiar to the senses is intimately related to the denominator of the fraction, viewed from the objective side. How far related, must next be discussed.

We must now shift our point of observation to the subjective centre; and here we are at once confronted by time and space. If we can apprehend these entities as Plato conceived them, we shall probably find the subjective complement of the Idea. And of the two entities, time and space, time, for reasons which we shall see, must be considered first.

The mutual relation of sensible phenomena is, according to Plato, the bare fact of antecedence and consequence, as it is conceived by Hume and Brown. That is to say, no reciprocal causal *nexus* prevails between the several sequents. A phenomenon A. passes into phenomenon B., through a point or stage of indifference, during which the *quantum* of elements is neither A. nor B. But we have seen that analysis resolves each member of the sequence into a new series of sequents, with *their* Point of Indifference; and so on to infinity. Now, Plato holds that at the point, or during the stage, of indifference, there is no phenomenon which sense can discover. The Point of Indifference determines phenomenon A.; but its successor, phenomenon B., has not yet appeared on the field. The Point of Indifference is, consequently, non-phenomenal. This is equivalent to saying that the Point of Indifference is not subject to the law of antecedence and consequence. Where there are no sequents, there can be no sequence.

But, in Plato's opinion, a state which is not subject to the law of antecedence and consequence is not subject to time. Time, strictly, in his opinion, is either past or future; that is, in abstract terms, either antecedence or consequence. The Point of Indifference is, therefore, non-temporal. Time, consequently, as Plato conceived it, is but a portion of the general fact of antecedence and consequence.

Each antecedent, as was said, merely precedes its consequent; each consequent merely succeeds its antecedent in the train; no one sequent exerts any causal influence on its neighbour. Further, the position of each member of the sequence may, relatively to other sequences, be completely reversed. A. is the antecedent to B. ; but A. may be the consequent to X., and B. may be the antecedent to Y. No antecedent or consequent, therefore, enjoys an independent plenary existence, but receives its temporary position from the mental apprehension of the Point of Indifference, the limiting principle of the Idea.

Plato, therefore, must have held—*first*, that Time properly denotes the actual members of a sequence, to the exclusion of the non-temporal Point of Indifference ; *second*, that the temporal members of a sequence could not have their actual transitional existence without the non-temporal Point of Indifference; and, *third*, that the actual members of a sequence do not during their phase of transition exercise any causal influence on each other. We may, accordingly, conclude that the transient or temporal matter of sensible phenomena was a subjective tendency only—a bare possibility of limitation by the Point of Indifference; and this conclusion is fully confirmed, as will be seen, by Plato's ethical views.

Time is thus exactly convertible with the sum of the *quasi*-individual sequents which make up the phenomenal universe, *minus* the Point of Indifference. But as each sequent is determined by the Point of Indifference, we thus get the notion of different lengths of phenomena, told off by the non-temporal point. These lengths are variously diversified by their contents, sensations of colour and resistance, and an abstraction of the contents gives us blank or undiversified time. Now, blank or undiversified time, is a mere negation. To recur to Plato's view of a judgment, blank time is a skeleton proposition, which has no actual existence save in the mind of its concipient. Blank time is usually made slightly positive by a reference to the most obvious phenomena, the motions of the sun and moon. Blank time is, accordingly, conceived as capable of containing any, but as actually containing no one phenomenon. The blank awaits the phenomenon, and the phenomenon involves the Idea. And this double suggestion of things conspicuous by their absence is, in Plato's opinion, the only real significance of the concept, pure space. As anything more than an expression in abstract of two propositions, pure space is, in Plato's opinion, a figment.[1] The *first* is, that the blank form, pure time, is a symbol of the possibility of a phenomenon which *eo ipso* denies its actuality. The *second* is, that the phenomenal sequence has the root of its being in the Idea.[2]

With respect to the particular modes of extension, Aristotle tells us that Plato used to grant the mathematical Point a hypothetic existence only, but that he fully recognised its value as the efficient of the Line.[3] Aristotle also states, that Two was the Number of the Line, Three of the Surface, and Four of

the Solid.' That is to say, a progression from point
A. to point B. is the Line; from A. to B., and
from B. to C., is the Surface; and from A. to B.,
B. to C., and then in another direction from C. to D.,
is the Solid. The Solid presupposes the Surface,
but not conversely; the Surface presupposes the
Line, but not conversely; and the Line presupposes
the Point, but not conversely. The basis of the
entire movement is the mathematical point; the
mathematical point is the monad localized; and the
monad localized is the Point of Indifference, with
the faintest reference to blank time. In other words,
the mathematical point is the Point of Indifference,
figured in the imagination. And these skeletons of
extension, clothed with the subjective material—resistance—are the tactual and muscular sensations of
modern psychology.

Whatever may be thought of Plato's analysis as
a contribution to philosophy, it is quite sufficient to
show his views as to the objectivity of Time and
Space. If Time be a portion only of sensible sequences, which expressly excludes the most important factor, and if space be but a portion of time,
it follows that time, and *à fortiori* space, in Plato's
opinion, cannot impart any objectivity to the sensible phenomena of which they are abstract fragments. But, as the various elements, with their
varying degrees of mobility or density, are functions
of subjective sensations, and of the Idea, it also
follows that, in Plato's opinion, there is no objec-

tive entity like matter—no mediating *tertium quid*—
between the psychic principle and the Idea. It follows also from this, that Time and Space, being
semi-sensuous, cannot be applied in any shape whatever to that which is purely supersensuous. In
positive language, the order of thought is the single
law of the noetic world.

We are now, perhaps, in a position to deal with
the Platonic technicality, Participation. If the preceding view of Plato's philosophy be sound, it is
obvious that all sensuous modes of conceiving that
process must be summarily set aside, as unfitted to
describe the objective relation of the Idea to the
psychic principle. As Ideas exist by participating
in The One,[*] so sensible things exist by participating in the Idea. Now, The One is the main element
of the Idea—the logical antecedent and efficient of
the completed combination. By parity of reasoning, the Idea is the main element of sensible perception—the logical antecedent and efficient of the
completed result. But, in Plato's opinion, combination denotes, not what may be called chemical,
but mechanical, composition. The elements reappear in the result unaltered. In and during the
combination, the elements preserve their individual
character, and their specific virtues. Participation,
in its technical sense, denotes, *first*, that the object
participated in is the more important member of the
union, both in logical dignity and in substantive independence; and, *second*, that each element preserves

its individuality unaltered, in and during its appearance in the joint effect of all the elements. The proposition that sensible things participate in the Idea signifies, therefore, *first*, that of the two elements of perception, subjective feeling and the Idea, the latter preponderates; and, *second*, that the two elements may be discovered side by side in the final process. To obviate misapprehensions, it cannot be too often repeated, that the terms elements and combination—process and results—relate only to the order of thought, and do not connote any mode of extension, or of empirical causation, whatsoever.* In positive language, Participation, therefore, signifies a process according to the order of thought, and nothing more. It may, perhaps, be rudely symbolized by the algebraic *plus*.

VII.

THE DEMIURGE OF THE TIMÆUS.

θοὼς δέ οἱ ἤνυτο ἔργον.
   Hom. *Od.* v. 243.

ARISTOTLE points out a discrepancy between the Timæus and the lectures of Plato.[1] The lectures of Plato appear to have been a systematic course, which he was in the habit of delivering. Some of them, at least, were of a highly abstruse and technical character. Various editions were published by several of Plato's most distinguished pupils, Aristotle amongst the rest. Leaving out of count Aristotle's lofty personal character, it is obvious that any misstatements would have been made in the face of numerous fellow-pupils and rival editors. But anyone really acquainted with Aristotle's works sees that it is almost an insult to his memory, to declare him incapable of misrepresentation. Aristotle's testimony, therefore, may be admitted without scruple.

The discrepancy between the lectures and the Timæus is, that in the former the vehicle of Participation was said to be The Indefinite—The Great, and The Small; while in the Timæus that function is assigned to space. The fact of *primâ facie*

discrepancy may be admitted at once. It may be
remarked, also, that Aristotle, here as elsewhere,
specially contrasts the Timæus with the general body
of Platonic doctrine. The Timæus, consequently,
is the only witness on Aristotle's side. But, as the
subjectivity of extension is a vital point in the views
advocated in this Essay, it remains to be considered
whether the discrepancy is ultimate, or not.

We must remember the historical position of
Plato's philosophy. Plato was an eclectic. His object was to elaborate a system of ethics by an amalgamation of the current forms of speculation. He
wished to reconcile the absolute unity of Parmenides with the relativity of Heracleitus. The medium
of reconciliation was the Numbers of Pythagoras.[1]

The various constituents of Platonism are represented in the Dialogues by a dramatic contrivance,
which has perhaps a nucleus of historical truth.
The negative or critical side in ethical argument is
generally conducted by Socrates, while the constructive part is intrusted to a disciple of a kindred
school. But the critical side of speculation is not
always negative in its results. The refutation of extreme sensualism necessitates the position of something supersensuous; and ethical problems do not
of necessity sound the depths of the metaphysical
gulf. Justice and Prudence, Temperance and Fortitude, Pleasure and Pain, are far more tangible objects than Existence and Unity. Besides, the purely

ethical problems are comparatively few in number,
when contrasted with the infinite varieties of metaphysical
construction. At all events, the credit of
the Platonic Socrates as an ethical expositor is not
involved in any metaphysical position, save the affirmation
of something at once supersensuous and
objective, and his reputation is thereby saved whole.
As a further instance of the same contrivance, the
delineation of the spiritual world is left to an Eleatic,
because Plato adopted as the foundation of his
system The One of Parmenides, who is always spoken
of with profound respect. But, as the Numbers of
Pythagoras were employed by Plato to connect the
intelligible One with the sensible Many, the exposition
of the relation between the two elements is
with great propriety put into the mouth of the
Pythagorean Timæus. We have seen that it is one of
the first principles of Platonism that elements in and
during their composition may be found unaltered;
and this notion Plato, with his usual artistic skill,
has embodied in the *rôles* of his various characters.
The Timæus of the Dialogue, accordingly, must be
held to convey Plato's own opinions in Pythagorean
language. Certain differences, however, between the
Numbers of Pythagoras and the Idea of Plato must
be kept in view, if we wish to render the sermon
of Timæus into its genuine Platonic equivalents.
But, as the complexion of the Timæus is highly
mythical, Plato's conception of a myth requires

some attention. Like everything in Plato, his conception of the myth is sharp and clear, and is the rigorous result of his peculiar opinions.*

It may be recollected, that according to Plato, every complex verbal symbol had its mental counterpart. A myth, consequently, is the duplicate of a mental state, and that state may be described somewhat as follows:—

Objectively, there is either existence, or there is not; objectively, there can be no compromise between the presence and the absence of reality. Subjectively, it is quite another thing. The judgment of the mind may, with reference to reality, be either true or false. Relatively to the object of knowledge, the cognitive principle may exist in three possible conditions. In the first, it is in full possession of objective reality—neither subject nor object exercising any mutual alterative influence. The direct antithesis of this is, when the cognitive principle is wholly wrapped up in the contemplation of one of its own creations, which it mistakes for objectivity. In the former state, the object is wholly objective; in the latter, wholly subjective. But between these two extremes a mean state is possible. The object of cognition may be partly objective, and partly subjective. We may discern substantial reality looming through the haze. To see the objective, as it is in its entirety, is (according to Plato), for reasons which we shall see, denied to man in his present state. To mistake the subjective modification for the objective reality, is the error of the majority of the sons of men. To be convinced that the subjective modification is not the objective reality, is the mean state of the Philosopher—the searcher for truth. The first state is the beatific condition of the perfect soul, and is termed by Plato divine. The second is compared by Plato to a dream, in which all sense of the outer world is lost. The intermediate condition is denoted by that term which signifies the state between sleep and waking, in which there is a slight sense of external things.[4]

Now, language is the reflex of thought; and thought, in Plato's opinion, is perpetually disturbed by the interruptions of the senses. Hence, the Philosopher, in endeavouring to describe his day-dreams, must employ the language of what may be termed the coma of the noetic faculty. In other words, he is obliged to describe that which is wholly non-temporal and unextended in phraseology modelled on a basis of Time and Space.

All sensation, according to Plato, is particular; there is no abstract sensation; every sensation must be a specific affection of a special organ. It must be, for example, colour; and colour must be green or blue, &c. The mimetic artist is, consequently, confined to particulars; sculptors and painters, more so, and poets less. The locks of the Phidian Zeus must have lain in some particular curves on the immortal brow. The artist in words has greater freedom. No sculptor could embody the wrathful

God descending Olympus in the gloom of outraged deity, nor communicate the awe breathed by the mere instruments of the coming vengeance, even before the deathless arm was exerted in destruction. No painter could set forth Achilles, as he shone in the heaven-sent glory on the brink of the bloody trench. And, though one man has by words done both, yet the conceptions actually employed are strictly sensuous details, which leave much to the imagination of the reader. The subjects, besides, are in reality sensuous. But in depicting what is wholly supersensuous in the colours of sense, we must have recourse either to extreme generality, and consequent faintness; or we may fill in the spiritual outlines with a profusion of details, which will show at once that the picture is meant to be symbolical. Plato has adopted the latter course; he elaborates his spiritual cartoons with almost wearisome minuteness. But, whatever may be thought of their merit as works of art, their significance as sensuous embodiments of spiritual reality is pretty evident. And nothing can well be harder than to turn Plato's precaution against misconception into an argument against his philosophical consistency. The spiritual world can only be depicted to the imagination in the special colours of sense, and the specialty of the colouring Plato has pushed to an extreme. Bearing this in mind, a Platonic myth may be defined to be, a description of supersensuous reality in the concrete language of the sensuous impression.

To use the Platonic metaphor, a myth is an account of the purely spiritual state of waking in the imagery of dreams, when the higher faculty is in total abeyance. In a word, the Platonic myth is parabolic, and not argumentative; and the myth differs from the parable only in the minute precision with which the smallest details are analogues of the unseen.

The mythical setting of the Timæus is to the following effect:—The Demiurge, or architectonic God, puts together the universe by joining three elements, viz :—the Noetic, the Sensible, and Space. These elements existed prior to the work of the Demiurge. The motive of the Architect was His own goodness, which He wished to impart to other intelligences. In pursuance of this end, and to give inferior beings an analogue or symbol of His own imperturbed eternity, the Demiurge contrived the celestial phenomena, in order that they might suggest the notion time. And, having committed the lower offices of elaboration to the mundane gods, the Architect rested from His work.

The differences between the Pythagorean Number and the Platonic Idea must be now adverted to. The numbers of Pythagoras were the parts which made up the sensible extended universe, and the universe was surrounded by infinite space. The numbers possessed extension, and bore somewhat the same relation to the Platonic Idea, that the modern conception of a force bears to its formula. The Number connoted extension. The Number was a mode of extension, while the Idea was pure intelligible essence, which existed aloof from any sensuous relation, even local position.³ This distinction being premised, the Timæus reads somewhat as follows :—

The motive of perfect and autonomous unity is goodness—the ultimate ethical aspect of personality. But the Perfect Personality is not a nebulous benevolence, which radiates its blessings indiscriminately on every side. Supreme Intelligence is its organon; and its work—the act of Divine Volition—shapes itself in harmony with Supreme Intelligence. But intelligence, though desirable on its own account—as an end—is also desirable as a step to something further—as a means. Intelligence, therefore, *quâ* means, is, in the order of thought, subsequent to perfection, which is exclusively an end. Now, the law of intelligence—the numerical index of the Idea—the numerator of the fraction—though logically subsequent to perfection, yet, *quâ* bare possibility, is prior to the undetermined activity, for the limitation of which it lays down the formula. An act of Divine volition is the means which brings the two extremes—Divine differentiating Intelligence, and Divine undifferentiated Substance—into harmony, and that harmony is the Idea. But, though the means of combination is subsequent in the order of thought to the things combined, the means is a *sine quâ non*. The Divine Efficient Will is the means of the combination of the Divine elements, and the Demiurge of the Timæus is that Will personified. The Demiurge —the architectonic God—is properly described, in the imagery of sense, as building the universe out of pre-existing elements, because the act of Divine personality is logically subsequent to its logical prerequisites—the intelligible or noetic formula, and the unexerted personal force. The Demiurge is, consesequently, Perfect Personality, apprehended in its Epiphany. The Demiurge is, therefore, distinct from the Good, the super-essential and absolute God. In other words, the Demiurge is an anthropomorphic conception of the Deity, in the act of submitting Himself to relation. And the Demiurge is said with strict dramatic propriety to build upon infinite space the fabric of the cosmical universe, because, the numbers of Pythagoras being modes of extension, extension as a pre-existing *tertium quid* was a necessity in the Pythagorean conception of the relation between the noetic and the sensible. According to the Pythagoreans, the universe was surrounded by infinite space. But Plato in the Timæus, as we shall see, expressly confines the functions of the figment space, to express two facts relating to the phenomenal scheme, viz :—the *quasi*-identity of each portion of a phenomenal series, and the real dependence of the entire sensible scheme upon its noetic basis. The Timæus, therefore, while it preserves dramatic and philosophical consistency, by admitting Space into a Pythagorean exposition of creation, in reality lays down the essential subjectivity of that notion. And we know from Aristotle that certain persons maintained the symbolism of the Timæus; that is, its covert noetic significance; and compared its functions to a mathematical diagram, which assists the apprehension of a theorem, while it very rudely denotes scientific exactness. These persons are said by Simplicius to be Speusippus and Xenocrates. Of these, Plato himself appointed his nephew Speusippus to succeed him as lecturer in the school. Speusippus had strong Pythagorean affinities, and was therefore not likely to underrate similar leanings in his immortal relative. And Xenocrates, who succeeded Speusippus, when the latter's health gave way, is pronounced by Simplicius to be the most staunch of Plato's immediate disciples. But, even without the express testimony of Simplicius, we might have inferred that the persons alluded to by Aristotle were the immediate successors of Plato in the school. We have, accordingly, contemporary testimony of the highest kind in favour of the symbolism of the Timæus.[*]

The Timæus is the stockpiece of those who see in Plato a metaphysician whose reason is overpowered by his imagination. To go into all the details of the Timæus would be entirely out of place, in a brief essay like the present; but there are two or three points which illustrate Plato's mode of thinking, and furnish a key to the dialogue.

The elementary bodies, according to the Timæus of the piece, are four, viz: Fire, Air, Water, Earth,

These are composed of triangles. The three first are compositions of different amounts of the same triangle. The last—Earth—is a compound of triangles of another order. The base of the three first elements is a right-angled triangle, whose hypotenuse is twice its lesser side. The base of the last element—Earth—is a right-angled isosceles triangle. Twenty-four of the elementary scalene triangles compose the Pyramid, the ultimate structural form of fire; forty-eight of the same triangles compose the Octahedron, the ultimate structural form of air; and one hundred and twenty of the same triangles compose the Icosihedron, the ultimate structural form of water. Twenty-four isosceles triangles compose the Cube, the ultimate structural form of earth. The union of all the various compounds is effected in the remaining solid—the ultimate structural base of the cosmical product. To understand this, we must have recourse, in the first place, to Plato's conception of mathematics; and, in the second, to the Pythagorean hypothesis of Number.'

The mathematical concepts, according to Plato, approach most nearly of human notions to pure noetic truth. It, however, they never reach; since they are, in fact, a combination of pure noetic existence with sensible extension; and the main element of extension is the sensuous indefinite. But as, in Plato's opinion, every element of a combination, in and during that combination, preserves its specific qualities unaltered, each element of the mathematical concept preserves its original characteristics. Hence no mathematical figure is ever perfect. The indefinite is always to be found in its true character therein. For example, the concrete circle is a mere approximation to the perfect circle, from which it is a falling off. The colouring matter of the sensuous agglomerate prevents the noetic nucleus from being seen in its natural transparency.

Of mathematical figures, the circle is the type of complete noetic reality; as the circle is bounded by a single line without beginning or end. In Platonic language, the circle of all figures partakes most of the Limit. But the antithesis of the Limit is the Unlimited, which as such is incogitable; to be construed to thought, it must be treated with some slight tincture of limitation. The infinite right line is, consequently, the best type of the Indefinite. But, as ancient arithmetic and geometry were closely allied—the several notions of arithmetical addition and of geometrical construction not having as yet attained their modern distinctness—the square—the right line multiplied by itself—is the type of the most marked antithesis to that which the circle typifies. Hence, the earth—the least moveable of elements—is denoted by the square; and its structural solid is the square multiplied by the right line—the cube. For we have seen that a line thrown off a surface is, in Plato's mode of thinking, the solid. The square, therefore, multiplied by the right line, is the cube. The word multiply is not strictly accurate, but Greek arithmetic had not attained the abstractness of the modern science. It would be nearer the mark to say that the square and its side are the factors of the cube.

The least moveable of the elements being denoted by the square, the most moveable is denoted by the circle; the curve and the right line being, according to the Pythagoreans, contraries of their kind. The circle and the square appear at first sight to have no medium of amalgamation. Such a medium is, however, afforded by the right-angled scalene triangle, whose hypotenuse is twice its lesser side. This will be seen from the annexed diagram. The

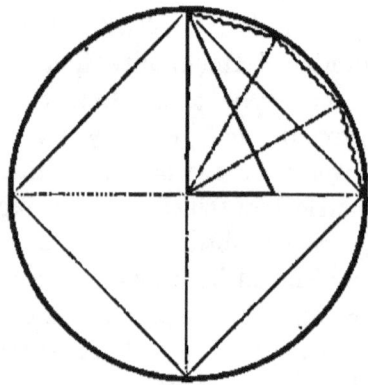

Circle, Square, and Triangle represent the constituents of the Idea. The Circle is the Limit; the Square is the Unlimited; and the scalene Triangle is their Indifference. The scalene Triangle is the basis of amalgamation; for, the angle at the centre being trisected,

the zigzag lines joining the trisectors denote that
the sides of the Dodecagon are bisectible to infinity,
and consequently the lines joining the bisectors to the
containing radii. In this way the Dodecagon approximates to the Circle, which it never reaches. The
right-angled scalene Triangle is the basis of compromise between the extremes, the Circle and the
Square—between fire and earth. For, as its greatest angle is right, it so far savours of the Square;
and as its least angle is one third of a right angle,
it contains the particular angle which brings the
Square into definite relation to the Circle. Now,
Three was the Pythagorean Number of the Definite;
and the triangle is its symbol, clothed with extension. Hence, the scalene Triangle in question is,
according to Plato, the most beautiful of figures. It
is also plain from the diagram that the right-angled
scalene Triangle is not a factor of the Square.
Practically speaking, the entire diagram may be obtained by constructing an equilateral Triangle, and
joining any one of its sides, produced to double its
original length, with the opposite angle, and then
describing the Circle. But such a construction exactly inverts Plato's mode of thought. The Triangle
presupposes both the Square and the Circle in
the order of thought; but the converse does not
hold.*

To understand the primitive forms of the various
elements, we must have recourse to the Pythagorean

Numbers. The Pythagorean Number was a formula and a force enclosed in a mode of extension. The Pythagorean Number was not a symbol; it was at once the "Impulse and the Law" of the sensible impression. In the Pythagorean system Four was the formula and force of the Solid—in modern abstract language, of impenetrability: wherever solidity was present, the Four was there. The Number Six was the formula and force of Life—in modern abstract language, of motivity. Motivity, 6, and impenetrability in its lowest power, 4, are the factors of Fire. It will be recollected that the right-angled scalene Triangle is the compromise between the Circle and the Square—the first actual combination of the two ultimate elements. The scalene triangle, consequently—the primordial base multiplied by motivity and impenetrability—gives us twenty-four Triangles—the structural units of the Tetrahedron, or Pyramid, the Solid allocated by the Demiurge to Fire.[*] Each side of this and of the other Solids (except the Cube), is an equilateral Triangle, consisting of six of the scalene Triangles, all the angles contained by the hypotenuse and lesser side pointing inwards.

The Number Eight was the formula and force of Love; that is, in modern abstract language, of affinity. Motivity, 6, and affinity, 8, are the factors of Air—air differing less than water from fire, and differing less than fire from water. But, as $6 \times 8 = 48$,

18 elementary triangles are the structural units of the Octahedron, the Solid allocated by the Demiurge to Air.[10]

The Number Five was the formula and force of Colour; in modern abstract language, of Quality. Motivity, 6, colour, 5, and impenetrability, 4, are the factors of Water. Water, according to Plato, was semi-visible, and semi-invisible; water, also, in the concrete language of ancient philosophy, denoted indefinite flux. Hence, in Platonic language, water partook much of the Indefinite. Now 4, which is 2×2, was the Pythagorean Number of the Solid; that is, in arithmetico-geometrical language, the square of the Indefinite. Two was the Number of the Indefinite, and corresponded to the Platonic More and Less —The Great and The Small—the Indefinite Dyad, ascribed by Aristotle and his commentators to Plato. Since, then, motivity, 6, $\times$ colour, 5, or quality or appearance, $\times$ the square of the Indefinite, $4 = 120$, 120 primitive scalene triangles are the structural units of the Icosihedron, the Solid allocated by the Demiurge to Water.

The fourth element—Earth—had a different origin. Its structural unit was the isosceles triangle, four of which produced the square—the Indefinite, 2, multiplied by itself. But, as the essential character of earth is impenetrability, its root is four; and four multiplied by motivity gives us twenty-four isosceles triangles, the structural units of the Solid allocated by the Demiurge to Earth. The Solids allocated to Fire and Earth, respectively, are aggregates of twenty-four structural units. But in the case of fire the root or main factor is motivity, of which solidity is the power; while in the case of earth the root is solidity, of which motivity is the power. The structural formation of the four elements, as described by Timæus, is strictly, therefore, in accordance with what we know of the Pythagorean numbers; and the basis of three structures, the scalene Triangle, is the third member of the Platonic Idea—the Indifference of the two Extremes. Taking into consideration Plato's principle, that all sensible objects, and therefore all sensible descriptions, must be definite and minute, we can read in the exposition by Timæus a perfect illustration of Plato's mathematical conception of physics couched in Pythagorean language. This will appear more clearly as we proceed.

As to the remaining Solid, Plato, in the Timæus, says that the Demiurge used it in the construction of the whole, compounded of the four elements. In the Epinomis, the elements are set down as five in number, and arranged as follows:—First comes fire; its extreme antithesis is earth. Midway come, in the order of precedency, æther, air, water. Of these three, æther is most, and water least, akin to fire. Fire represents the Principle and Law of Limitation, and earth the Indefinite Receptivity; and these two elements reappear in the most fiery and least earthy compound, æther; and in the most earthy and least fiery compound, water; and in the compound which is the indifference of both, air. Now, as, according to Plato, all sensible objects are definite—since there is no abstract general existence—it follows that there is no sensible Cosmus apart from the sum total of its several elements. But as, according to the Pythagoreans, the sensible universe was an aggregate of number, the most noetic solid is allocated by Timæus to the structure of the whole. Of the five solids, the Dodecahedron approximates most nearly to the Sphere. The fifth solid, the Dodecahedron, is allocated by Xenocrates to the fifth element, æther. Now, æther was, in physical language, the most fiery; in mathematical language, the most spherical; and, in strict Platonic language, contained the largest noetic constituent. But, as the noetic element is the Principle and Law of Limitation, and as the essence of limitation is totality, it follows, that the fifth remaining solid, which, in the more concrete language of the Pythagorean Timæus, is allocated to the whole, is properly the physical symbol of the least physical compound of Limitation and the Indefinite. Again, then, by reading the Timæus as an exposition of Platonism, in Pythagorean concrete imagery, we are able, without the slightest straining of the text, to vindicate the consistency of Plato. The above view is also, as was said, confirmed by the high authority of Xenocrates, whom Simplicius calls the soundest of Plato's pupils; and here closes the *a priori* argument, which of course only shows that the Timæus *may be* a Pythagorean reading of Platonism. The following arguments will, it is conceived, verify the *a priori* probability, and show that it must be so construed.

Extension, we have seen, was a *sine quâ non* in the Pythagorean scheme; the universe floated in infinite space. We have the express testimony of Aristotle showing that Plato denied all locality to the Idea. All the objections which are urged by Aristotle against the Idea savour of locality. Deny Aristotle's assumption of necessary extension, and all his objections come to nothing. Plato has himself, in the Parmenides, urged the very same objections against all material modes of conceiving the relation between the Idea and sensible things. Therefore, in Plato's opinion also, the localization of the Idea was fatal to its existence. And yet, in the same dialogue, Parmenides asserts that the interests of the higher philosophy are bound up in the existence of the Idea. We are therefore forced to conclude, either that Plato spent his life in teaching, and appointed his relatives and friends to teach after his death, what he had himself most clearly proved to be absurd, or that he did not hold the objectivity of space. That Plato did not always, or perhaps often, set forth all his premises, we have his own authority and example for holding; but that he deliberately taught what he knew to be false, is utterly incredible. We must therefore, hold that Plato denied the objectivity of Space.

But this is not all. Plato, in the Timæus, expressly tells us that Space did not exist on earth or in heaven. In abstract language, that Space was neither the object of a sensible impression, nor of noetic intuition. Neither is Space an object of that natural belief which is part of the sensible impression. It is the creature of an illicit process of reasoning; its double function, as an abstract of phenomenal *quasi*-identity, and of phenomenal dependence, exhausts the small modicum of reality which it contains. But, as these two points are sufficiently provided for by the main body of Platonic doctrine, it follows that, even in the Timæus, objectivity is denied to Space. But to deny the objectivity of Space is tantamount to denying the essentially Pythagorean character of the Timæus.

The analysis of the notion Time yields similar results. Aristotle tells us that, according to the Pythagoreans, the number Three was the formative principle of the universe, and of each of its parts.[11] Aristotle likewise points out the objective character, in their eyes, of the Triad, which he translates into the more fruitful terms, Beginning, Middle, and End. Now, according to the Timæus, the universe was not created in time. Time is a consequence of creation, and not its prerequisite, either logical or substantive. In other words, the term time is of narrower extent than the sum of sensible sequences. Time, according to Plato, is not properly a subjective form, which regulates and alters sensible appearances. It is but a portion of the compound, made up of the subjective Indefinite, and the objective Idea. Further, in the Timæus, the modes of time are limited to two—the past and the future; and the present is a glimpse of eternity. Consequently, Plato, in his Timæus, does not admit the coequal importance of the three members of the Triad. The Timæus, therefore, does not teach the true Pythagorean doctrine of the Triad; that is, of the law of antecedence and consequence. The Timæus strongly enunciates the fact of the mere transitory or *quasi*-identity of each member of a phenomenal sequence, and the fact of the dependence of all such sequences upon a noetic basis. Now, all the parts of time must be wholly objective, or wholly subjective, or partly both. All the parts of time, according to the Pythagoreans, were equally objective. The first hypothesis is negatived by the express statements of the Timæus, and so likewise is the second. It follows, of necessity, that the Timæus teaches the genuine Platonic doctrine, that a sensible sequence is composed of a temporal, and a non-temporal or objective element. The Timæus, therefore, must be regarded as a myth, which generally conveys, in Pythagorean language, the rationale of the noetic to the sensible, but which expressly teaches the genuine Platonic doctrine of time and space.

Another point in the Timæus requires some consideration. The Demiurge is represented as in constant conflict with necessity, which he only partially overcomes. The Demiurge's constructions are but *quam proxime* attempts. They are never completely successful. But this apparent Sabæism is merely a mythical picture of the several constituents of the Idea. Between the members of a sensible sequence, according to Plato, no causal *nexus* prevails. Each antecedent melts insensibly into its consequent. The regulative and formative efficient of the series is the Point of Indifference. That is to say, on the one hand we have the unifying noetic Monad—the formula, and in part the impulse, of the series. Its antithesis—ununified Indefinite—as such, is incogitable. To be construed to thought, the Indefinite must be subjected to limitation. But the Indefinite of the sensible universe contains two elements—the subjective sensuous indefinite, and the objective Indefinite of the Idea. It is also, we have seen, a principle of Plato's, that elements remain unaltered by composition. Thus, in the junction of the unifying Monad with The Indefinite, each element preserves its specific virtue. The Indefinite, consequently, is still discoverable in the combination as an indispensable logical antecedent. Hence, the Demiurge—the means of combination personified—does not reduce either element to non-entity. As the logical and substantive means of combination, he persuades the consequent to submit to its antecedent, without forfeiting its individuality. The Demiurge

"Mollitque animos, et temperat iras,"

of the opposing elements.

The relation between the sensible element of a series and its noetic point throws light upon a curious myth in the Politicus. The providential God occasionally lets go the helm of the universe, and retires to his look-out. The subordinate Gods upon this immediately quit their posts, and the progress of the universe is suspended; and then things begin to move in the contrary direction. In the days of King Cronus, the recession of things was the normal condition; under Zeus, progress is the law, subject, however, to temporary suspension, and consequent recession. Under Cronus, old men ceased to grow older, and then grew young, and before their final exit became infants; and corpses after a little wholly disappeared. Human beings, and what are now the products of human invention, were yielded by the earth. All the great convulsions of the sensible universe are caused by the temporary withdrawal of the Providential God, and the consequent development of the retrogressive tendency inherent in things.

In the Philebus two methods of logical procedure are pointed out: we may proceed either upwards from The Indefinite to the Monad, or downwards from the Monad to The Indefinite.[13] In the former method we pass from the sensible to the noetic; in the latter, from the noetic to the sensible. In the latter case, that member of the series which is nearest to the noetic point is naturally prior to that which is further off. Hence, that which is next the noetic point becomes the antecedent, and therefore all the other members are its consequents. The order of the same series is completely reversed, according as our observation is taken from the noetic, or the sensible centre. The observation from the sensible centre is the ordinary one, under the present *regime* of Zeus. Under Cronus things were looked at from the noetic point—the point nearest Uranus, the purely noetic monarch. But, as extreme and almost ludicrous particularity is of the essence of the Platonic myth, the noetic order is translated into the concrete imagery of particular cases of the general law: for example, old men became young. And things are said to be produced from the earth—the symbol of the Indefinite—because, in descending from the noetic point, the Indefinite is the lowest step, upon reaching which, we begin the converse process of ascent; and the recession, consequent on the withdrawal of the Divine steersman, means, that the noetic non-temporal point is the main factor of the series, in the absence of which it comes to an abrupt close. In that case, as before, the last consequent—the completion of the series—is, from the opposite point of view, considered to be its beginning. Hence the myth in the Politicus.

From these, as well as from the other Platonic myths, we may grasp Plato's notion of sensible appearances. Sensible appearances bore to plenary noetic reality the relation which a sign bears to the thing signified. Sensible appearances were the symbols—"The alphabet"—of the spiritual significates; and for this view we have the very highest authority—an argumentative passage in the Parmenides. The notions that sensible things *resemble* their objective archetypes, either in whole or in part, is fully refuted by the Parmenides of the Dialogue.[13] Resemblance involves a recession to infinity. The notion that the relation of a sign to its significate is one of either total or partial similarity is still fruitful in the polemics of modern metaphysics. Upon the notion that significancy involves at least partial similarity is based Sir W. Hamilton's misconception of Brown's theory of perception. M. Cousin's criticism of Locke's theory of knowledge rests on the same assumption. But we have an older example of the same notion. Aristotle criticizes the mythical epilogue of the Phædo in the same spirit, and as seriously, as he criticizes the Idea of The Good;[14] and this brings us to Aristotle's point of view of Platonism.

In the language of the present day, Aristotle's philosophy was a mixture of the psychology of common sense and of the empirical view of physics. Aristotle postulated both in ethics and in psychology a healthy state of the media of perception. This being granted (which, of course, slurs over the whole point at issue between Plato and the Heracleitans) Aristotle lays down his canon of objectivity:—"That which seems to all, that, we say, is."[15]

This short sentence contains three distinct propositions, none of which Plato would have admitted, and to contradict which, was the fixed purpose of his long life. In the first place, the opinion of all men had nothing whatever to do with the question. All men may be wrong; and, according to Plato, no man could in his present condition see the entire truth in any given case. In the second place, that which *seemed* might or might not be irreconcileable with plenary reality. The appearance might or might not correctly symbolize reality, but could never be similar to it, and, *a fortiori*, never identical with it. And, in the last place, were Seeming and Reality identical, Plato considered that Heracleitus had made good his case. But Aristotle, taking the concrete sensible impression to be the ultimate unit of perception, and disregarding the antinomy which Plato professed to see, consistently attached at least equal necessity to space and time, which were essential adjuncts of the impression. Hence, Aristotle urges against the hypothesis of Ideas objections which assume that these entities are, or at least ought to be, subject to time and space. The Idea, according to Aristotle, has no motive power; and it is not, on Plato's own showing, the Primum Movens. The Idea, consequently, ought to have been subject to space. But Plato's conception, of noetic Rest and of noetic Motion, has been already dwelt on.

The Timæus may, accordingly, be considered as illustrating in a remarkable manner two of Plato's tenets. The first is, that every sensation is particular—there is no abstract phantom sensation. The second is, that the scheme of sensible appearances is a set of symbols, which may denote noetic reality. From these symbols we obtain the abstractions time and space. But even of these abstractions, the main element is noetic; and the subjective contingent cannot be understood, unless from the point on the basis of which Plato constructed his system of ethics.

VIII.

JUSTICE.

Οἱ αὑτῷ κακὰ τεύχει ἀνὴρ ἄλλῳ κακὰ τεύχων·
Ἡ δὲ κακὴ βουλή τῷ βουλεύσαντι κακίστη.
Hes. *Op. et D.* I. 263-4

The scope of Plato's philosophy was essentially ethical. His object was to set ethics upon a transcendental basis. He wished to connect the scheme of morality, which, he thought, ought to prevail between man and man, with the Divine Personality. It is, consequently, *a priori* likely that the exact significance of the Idea—the peculiar feature of Plato's philosophy—will be best realized by a study of the Platonic ethics.

The conception which underlies the Platonic ethics is the supposed analogy between the science and art of conduct, and a special trade or craft. To make the analogy perfect, each analogue requires a worker, a task, and an implement. The notion from which analysis disengages the ethical operator, his apparatus, and his task, is conduciveness, or fitness for a special purpose. The fitness of an implement indicates its use; and the stress of the argument, in each case, rests on the more or less special fitness of the given means to its supposed end.

The human agent is capable of two opposite courses of conduct towards both human and Divine natures. A certain course of conduct towards man is termed just; and the opposite is unjust. A certain course of conduct, considered relatively to the Deity, is termed holy; and this conduct has its contrary likewise. The generic terms which comprehend the species are Virtue and Vice. To use the language of the Platonic analogy, virtue is the efficiency of the agent in performing the task which the concurrent existences—man and God—directly or indirectly impose. Vice is, to continue the analogy, that inefficient condition in which the operator performs his allotted task, either carelessly or not at all.

In at least one respect the psychic principle, or human agent, is superior to every instrument. It can see itself at work, and can accordingly estimate and register its own progress or declension in moral efficiency. The power of self-cognition involves the several notions of a subject, an object, and their mutual relation. If there be something which knows, there must be something which is known; and if there be something which knows, and something which is known thereby, a relation is, *eo ipso*, established between them. The analogy is thus perfect. The subject is the producer of conduct; the object is the conduct produced; and the mutual relation of the two extremes is that condition of the agent which is instrumental in producing the conduct in question. There are, therefore, in ethics at least three problems. *First,* What is the state of the agent, when he is regarded as the efficient of his own conduct? *Second,* What is the aspect which the same conduct presents, when duly estimated by the agent himself, or by beings either similar or in some degree analogous? And, *third,* What is the bilateral relation between the agent and his work.

1. *The Ethical Subject.*

The first problem in Ethics is to determine the state of the agent with reference to various courses of conduct. That problem can, in Plato's opinion, only be solved by psychological data—by a reference to psychic fact. Plato's psychology divides psychic facts, for ethical purposes, into two grand categories, which correspond to the rational and the non-rational elements of Aristotle.[1] To borrow another illustration from arithmetic, the psychic principle is an integer, which analysis divides into fractions. The preponderating fraction is the rational element. The non-rational residue is made up of the emotional portion of our nature and of the appetence. The emotional fraction contains the emotive or impulsive moiety of the Will, as well as the sentimental feelings of modern psychology. The appetence is a tendency to all objects which either directly or indirectly produce sensual pleasure, or relieve or ward off sensual pain. The appetence, accordingly, includes all the mental states arising from the notion, property and its modifications. The three fractions—Reason, Emotion, and Appetence—are for ethical purposes to be considered as distinct. The principle upon which their distinctness is based is, according to Plato, the fact that the same extrinsic object may evoke opposite tendencies in the same individual at the same instant. The contrary tendencies, accordingly, require distinct names.[1] This is the psychological basis of the Platonic ethics.

The sub-fraction Appetence is a complex psychic state. In its more important variety, the bodily appetites, physical pain is the state which suggests the notion of its specific remedy. Hunger, for example, is painful; and hunger suggests the notion of relief by means of food. With the notion of the means of relief is associated the pleasure arising from its use. The appetites, therefore, are complex states, consisting of the notions pain, its remedy, and the consequent relief.[2] In other, and less practically important cases, such as colour and smell, bodily pain is not the necessary condition of pleasure. The former species of gratification Plato calls Mixed Pleasure, as pain is its condition precedent; the latter he terms Pure, as it is wholly unalloyed with pain. In either case Appetence finds its pleasures in its specific object, without any regard to the circumstances which may attend the gratification of its wants.[4]

But, though Appetence is a blind tendency towards its specific object, the circumstances which attend its gratification may become the object of another set of feelings. A man may be displeased with himself for having gratified some appetite on some particular occasion, when at other times the very same gratification evokes no feeling of disapprobation whatsoever. The former state of mind is classed by Plato under the emotive or irascible element, which in this case denotes the subjective sanction of morality—the pains of conscience. And the fact, that there is an emotional or sentimental aspect of morality, is the element of truth which gives vitality to the modern theory of a moral sense. But, in all cases of moral displeasure, it is the circumstances attending such gratification, and not the gratification pure and simple, which evoke the feeling. Now, the question of the particular circumstances in any given case is to be dealt with by the reason only. And the reason, according to Plato, can only act as follows:—The reason adds up the various *items* of the pleasures and pains resulting from the whole transaction, and strikes a balance between them. The emotive penalty attaches only when the balance is on the side of pain, and when the appetite has been expensively gratified. But, if the balance be in favour of pleasure, the pains of conscience are not evoked.⁵

It must not be forgotten that the objects of the Appetence include, according to Plato, not only the immediate objects of the several senses, but also the aggregate of rights and duties which are founded thereon. It must likewise be remembered, that the distinction, between the gratification itself and the specific circumstances which attend it, is equally important in the objects of immediate and mediate utility. Hence, the calculation of *items* covers the entire field of social, legal, and political duties, as well as the so-called duties to one's-self. The state of the agent relatively to his task is one of calculation, and his errors attract a self-inflicted, self-exacted penalty. To pursue the Platonic metaphor, the calculating machine registers its own aberrations. Morality, from the subjective point of view, is regarded by Plato as a branch of the art of computation. His opinion of the relation of each computation to the Divine nature will be seen in the course of the Section.

2. *The Ethical Object.*

The second question is, What are the characteristics of the ethical object? We have seen that the ethical subject is calculating power. The ethical object, therefore, must be the items of the calculation. We require, consequently, a *catalogue raisonnée* of the ethical items; and the next question is, Who is qualified to compile it?

Plato answers, the Philosopher—the seeker after truth. The Philosopher alone has experienced the pleasures of satisfied intelligence, of satisfied emotion, and of satisfied sense. He alone can depose to the entire case. The other witnesses—the man of ambition, and the man of business—can only give their experiences of their own specialty; but the Philosopher has tried their pleasures, along with others which are all his own. The Philosopher, consequently, is the person to draw up the catalogue.⁶

But the testimony of the Philosopher is not a statement of his own subjective feelings merely. His testimony is founded in part on the objective characteristics of the three orders of pleasures. The pleasures of Appetence are all subject to the law of antecedence and consequence. Relatively to their immediate antecedent, the pleasures of Appetence are, we have seen, either pure or mixed. The mixed pleasures—the most violent enjoyments of sense—are preceded by sensual pain. The pure pleasures, which are of a milder order, are not so preceded. Relatively to their immediate consequent, some pleasures of Appetence are followed by pain, and others not. Even granting that all pleasures, *quâ* pleasures, are equally pleasures, without reference to their consequents, it is a fact that certain pleasures are followed by pain in the order of sequence. We are, therefore, forced to draw a distinction between pleasures according to the peculiarities of their consequents. Relatively to both antecedents and consequents, the following is, therefore, the precedency of the various phenomenal pleasures:—First, pure pleasure; that is to say, pleasure neither preceded nor followed by pain. Second, mixed pleasure—pleasure which, though preceded, is not followed by pain. Third, pleasure both preceded and followed by pain. Of these the first alone—pleasure neither preceded nor followed by pain—Plato placed in the hierarchy of Good, wherein it occupies the lowest grade.[1] To the second the Philosopher would conform as far as is absolutely necessary, and no further. The third he must rigidly eschew.

The pleasures of the higher faculties occupy a very different position. All the pleasures of Appetence are of the sensible Indefinite; they are subject to the law of antecedence and consequence. But from this law, noetic reality stands entirely aloof, being subject only to the law of the order of thought. The object of the noetic faculty is Reality, apprehended by the reason as Truth, and by the emotive element as of the nature of the Good. But, though neither truth, nor, *a fortiori*, the Good can be adequately apprehended by man in his present abject condition, yet the slightest glimpse of reality altogether surpasses the fullest enjoyment of phenomenal pleasures. Hence the Philosopher—the seeker after reality—ranges the ethical items on the side of Good, as follows:—First, noetic reality; Second, *longo intervallo*, pure phenomenal pleasures. On the side of evil there is but one item—phenomenal pleasure both preceded and followed by pain. But the pain is not the sole, nor even the chief, reason why the latter pleasures are denounced by Plato as bad. Why they are so, will be seen further on. Here it may be remarked, that the Good is of much wider range than its contrary, as it is the object of the noetic faculty, and of the higher phenomenal tendencies, while the province of evil is confined to the third species of phenomenal pleasure. The second species of phenomenal pleasure is to be submitted to under protest; it is, in itself, neither good nor bad.

3. *The Relation between the Ethical Subject and Object.*

The third Ethical problem is, What is the relation between the moral calculator and the moral items? Its solution is furnished by the Platonic notion of Beauty.

The psychic principle is, we have seen, the indissoluble combination of cognitive power and emotive tact. To the cognitive faculty—reason—things are presented under the relation of means and ends. But those objects which reason regards as means to some specific end, in proportion to their perfection as means, appeal to the emotive element as ends. For it is of the nature of emotion to regard what-

ever evokes it as its end and aim. Nor is this view
without the sanction of the reason. Reason sees
that an infinite series of means is an absurdity.
Reason, in other words, sees that there must be an
end of some kind or other, although its particular
features are not at the moment discernible. Hence,
reason accepts the deliverances of the emotive element, which thus become indirectly objects of cognition. And that object, which on the one hand is
apprehended by the reason directly as a Means, and
indirectly as an end; and which, on the other hand,
appeals to the emotive element wholly as an end, is
what Plato calls the Beautiful—the perfect Indifference of Means and of End.*

We have seen that the psychic principle was regarded by Plato as a piece of machinery working to
a specific end. The moral calculator keeps an account of the moral items, and on his efficiency as a
calculator depends his moral wealth. Efficiency,
therefore, is the notion which brings into harmony
the correlative but distinct notions of the calculator
and his items. In the order of thought, the items
to be calculated presuppose the calculator, but the
converse does not hold; and calculating efficiency
presupposes both, but not conversely.

Now, the notion efficiency is strictly a relation
between means and end. Efficiency, consequently,
in Platonic language, partakes of the Beautiful.
The efficiency of the ethical instrument is one
amongst other beautiful things. But, as the power

of self-cognition is inseparable from the psychic
principle, the psychic principle can see itself at work,
and observe the adaptation of intrinsic means to intrinsic ends. Now, according to Plato, the adaptation of ethical means to ethical ends, in proportion
to its perfection, evokes in the subject the complex
state of reason and emotion acting in sympathy.
That is to say, a state of the agent may appear beautiful to himself, and consequently be a phase of the
most exalted pleasure. Hence, then, that state is desirable as a means to that end. But the Platonic
name for intrinsic efficiency is Justice. Justice is,
therefore, desirable as a means to that end.

Efficiency is also desirable, as the only means
which secures that end. For, while Efficiency is regarded by the reason directly as a means, Efficiency
is to the emotive element wholly an end. Efficiency
is also recognised by reason as the special choice of
the emotion, and as a case of the more general principle, that the notion means implies the notion end.
Efficiency, relatively to the subject's own internal
condition, is therefore desirable both as a means
and as an end. But this is Plato's thesis in the
Republic with regard to Justice.

As the state of Efficiency relates, as will be seen,
to the noetic faculty, it is obvious that it cannot be
destroyed by any phenomenal disturbance, save what
comes from itself. But, as other agents can produce
only phenomenal disturbance, it follows that no ill-
will on the part of other agents can reach the agent's

own noetic aptitude. It is self-maintained, and can only be self-destroyed. Hence, one man can intercept the legal and social utilities which accrue to another from the senses and their objects ; but his Power stops here. The inner Efficiency of the agent no other being can touch.⁹

But the utility of Efficiency reaches further. Admiration, being once awakened in the subject by a contemplation of his self-developed excellence, is naturally extended to all analogous excellences. Hence, all moral and intellectual excellence becomes the object of its impassioned sentiment. The highest degree of fervour is raised by the contemplation of the Supreme Excellence, which is presented to us *now* as a means—as the efficient of Beauty and Utility, and as the ground of Truth and Existence. But in this capacity the Divine Nature, *quà* means, necessarily involves, as a correlative end, an ulterior and absolute excellence, still more admirable.¹⁰

In every case where the agent renders himself capable of appreciating excellence in others, he *eo ipso* attracts their reciprocal love and admiration, as soon as his excellence is brought within their cognisance. Efficiency thus elicits the agent's own admiration ; it leads him to admire kindred excellence in others, and procures him in return their sympathetic and responsive love. And this state of the psychic principle, considered in relation to its subject and to all its possible objects, is the Platonic Eros.

Justice, therefore, is desirable in itself and in its consequences. Justice is desirable as an end, as it is a phase of the most exalted pleasure. Justice is desirable as a means, as it is the only means of attracting the impassioned love of kindred beings, and the crowning sympathy of Supreme Perfection.

We now, perhaps, see that the notion Beauty is the key of the Platonic ethics. The ethical subject is computing or calculating power; the ethical object is the sum of the items; and the two notions are correlated by the mean notion, calculating Efficiency. Calculating efficiency as an end is the first item in the account, and as a means it brings the other items into computation. Each item is a step, and the only step to the next, and so on to the last. But, as each item is thus indifferently means and end, each item is, strictly speaking, beautiful.

4. *Ethical Training.*

In addition to the three problems which are inevitable in every system of ethics, a fourth question has engrossed a large portion of modern speculation —the Genesis of the moral notions. But this mode of stating the question inverts Plato's conception of the ethical faculty.

According to Plato, ethical efficiency is an automatic or spontaneous faculty, whose inherent activity is always at *par*, but whose movements may be impeded by certain obstructions. The tendency of modern speculation—which has received its impetus from Aristotle, rather than from Plato—is to regard the moral principle as a resultant of counteracting pressures, one of which can only gain in force what the other loses. The preponderant habit, whether virtuous or vicious, grows gradually stronger, until the counteracting force is reduced practically to zero. Now, Plato would admit that the disturbing force may vary in intensity, from complete preponderance to practical non-entity; he would likewise admit that the various perturbations owe their strength to habit; but he would at the same time maintain that the mischief is altogether due to the obstacles which impede the working of the moral faculty, and not to any weakness either natural or acquired in the faculty itself. The strong man is there in all his strength, but he is bound hand and foot. Ethical training is consequently, according to Plato, a process of removing the obstacles to the working of the moral faculty.

The root of this theory may be found in Plato's conception of the psychic principle. The psychic principle is, on a small scale, a counterpart of the Supreme Nature, and next to it in inherent dignity. The psychic principle consists of The One, the Indefinite and their Indifference, in the same way as the Idea. But, as the faculty of self-cognition pervades the entire psychic principle, the psychic principle sees itself to be an object, as well as a subject. But, as an object compounded of The One and the Indefinite, the psychic principle is an Idea.

In the highest state of the psychic principle, the noetic faculty would see the Idea in its entirety. By parity of reasoning, the last state would be not merely total ignorance of the Idea, as such, but an acquiescence in some one aspect of its manifold relations as the absolute reality, beyond which there is nothing to be known. Between the extremes of unimpeded intuition and a thoroughgoing sensualism, midway stands the Philosopher. The Philosopher submits to the senses *de facto*, and looks forward to the Ideal world, of which he now catches a very faint glimpse. But, although he cannot altogether shun the importunities of sense, he is able to see by a strenuous effort that their exactions are a burden to which his own feebleness alone gives weight. He cannot unsee the sensible; he cannot emancipate himself from time and space; but he is able to gather that these relations spring from his own imperfections. He also sees that the root of his imperfections is coeval with his birth. The body is a portion of phenomenal sequence, and may be psychologically regarded as the sum of cerebral successions to which we find ourselves attached. Like all other sequences, the body depends upon a noetic efficient, relatively to which it holds an inferior position, as a dependent on the plenary existence of its superior. The body, so far, is inferior to the psychic principle; and is so far imperfect, and so far evil. Ethical training, therefore, must consist in minimizing the influence of the senses—including in the latter term, not only their immediate objects, but also the mental notions attached thereto, such as property, &c., and all other rights and duties, legal, social, and political. Ethical efficiency is, consequently, at its height in the present state of things, when ethical training has reduced to a minimum the effect of all sensuous objects. And so, conversely, the worst state of the ethical subject is when habits of indulgence have maximized sensual influences. In either case the terms body or senses must, as has been observed, be understood to comprehend, not only all the objects of the appetites, but also all the rights and duties to which they give rise—in a word, all things in relation to sense. This is the meaning of Plato's view of the senses as the occasion of all moral evil.

The correlation in the objective Idea of The One and The Indefinite gives rise to actual limitation. So the correlation in the subject of The One and The Indefinite gives rise to actual limitation. But, as the psychic principle is an indissoluble combination of reason and emotion, the correlation of the psychic elements give rise to emotional, as well as rational limitation. Now, the ethical limit is Prudence; the ethical Indefinite is Appetence—Appetence denoting not merely desire for sensual pleasures, but also a shrinking from sensual pains. The state, accordingly, which correlates the extremes Prudence and love of sensual pleasure is Temperance; and the state which correlates Prudence and dread of sensual pain is Fortitude; and thus both virtues have for their object-matter bodily states. But, as the body, according to Plato, denotes, as was said, both the immediate objects of the senses, and all the rights and duties public and private founded thereon, and as these are the sole occasions of injustice and impiety, it follows that Temperance and Fortitude cover all the duties which we owe to other beings, Divine and human; and Temperance and Fortitude considered in immediate relation to the agent, and not with reference to other beings, converge in the one state, Justice." Justice, therefore, according to Plato, is secured by that course of conduct which minimizes sensual stimuli; and by minimizing sensual stimuli, we give the noetic faculty room to work.

The Platonic formula, that injustice is involuntary, is another mode of expressing the same doctrine. As sensuous influences are the only hindrances to complete noetic intuition, and as these are reduced by Justice to a minimum, the noetic faculty, intuition, must see the psychic state Justice in all its beauty. Seeing this, the agent must conform to Good. No one desires evil save as a means of procuring some end. The means are *ex hypothesi* evil, and are therefore phenomenal. They therefore relate to some phenomenal end. Since, according to Plato, phenomenal means may obstruct noetic efficiency, but cannot produce it, the noetic effect of phenomenal means is, in a word, negative. Hence, their positive producing power must be confined to phenomenal ends. But, as the influences of phenomenal ends are minimized by Justice, no one can desire the means of that end which has long since ceased to excite any interest in him; the end has lost all its attraction, and with it the means. But in the case of the greatest moral depravity, phenomenal means have become the sole ends of conduct. In this latter case the noetic faculty is totally obstructed; it cannot see Justice at all. The unhappy being has shut out the light—that he loves the darkness, is the worst phase of his disease. No one, therefore, is voluntarily unjust, any more than he is voluntarily mad. This will be seen more clearly when we come to Plato's theory of the will.

In the Republic, the purport of which is ethical,[12] the worst state of the individual is likened to the worst state of the body politic—tyranny. The analogous individual is said to be 729 times removed from the regal or ideally virtuous man.

The meaning of this appears to be as follows:— The noetic soul is wholly free from Appetence, and consequently from the subjective pains of conscience appended thereto. The cognitive faculty and the higher emotions, therefore, coexist in complete harmony. But, on earth, the psychic principle is connected with a series of sensible sequences. These sequences, viewed in their ethical relation to the psychic principle, constitute an Idea. On the one

side we have the controlling principle, prudence;
on the other, the controlled sequence, Appetence;
and the necessary correlation of both completes the
Idea. Hence, the perfect human being contains three
moments—prudence, appetence, and their correlation; and government would be carried on by that
individual for the good of the whole exclusively.
But, as no human being is perfect, even as a compound of reason and sense, it follows that the reason never in fact is supreme. Its dictates are always modified by the suggestions of sense; that is to
say, sense, in place of being wholly a subject, becomes a part sovereign. But sense, being, according
to Plato, Indefinite, cannot either as subject, or part
sovereign, be construed to thought without some
admixture of Limitation. Hence, the sovereign contains three moments—Reason, Appetence, and consequent Indifference, and so likewise the subject. But,
as was before stated, Greek arithmetic was geometrical in conception and in expression. Numbers, in
relation to one another, were conceived as generating surfaces and solids. Consequently, the relation
of the three moments of the sovereign to the three
moments of the subject was represented by the rectangle under 3 and 3, by $3 \times 3 = 9$. Consequently nine
denoted what Plato calls Timocracy—a state of the
individual and of the body politic in which the
sovereign acts generally, but not always, for the
good of the whole body aggregate or sole.

Of the Timocracy the antithesis is Oligarchy—

the state of the individual and the body politic in which the sovereign acts for the aggrandizement of its order, and makes the interest of the subject subordinate thereto. That is to say, a fresh contingent of Appetence—the love of material power—is added to the sovereign element. Hence, the sovereign of the Timocracy being 3, and the new contingent being 3, $3 \times 3 = 9$; and, the subject being 3 as before, $9 \times 3 = 27$—the number which denotes the shortcomings of the Oligarchy, aggregate and sole.

Of the two extremes, Timocracy and Oligarchy, the compromise is Democracy. Democracy partakes of Timocracy, so far as it is sometimes influenced by high and noble motives, and of Oligarchy, so far as it pursues a course of selfish aggrandizement. Hence, the Democratic sovereign is denoted by the governing 3 of the Timocracy, and by the governing 9 of the Oligarchy. But, as $3 \times 9 = 27$, and as the subject is 3, as before, $27 \times 3 = 81$, the number which denotes the shortcomings of the Democracy, aggregate and sole.

These three polities are not actuated by mere immediate utility; all of them, more or less, have ulterior objects, and regard the good of the subject-body, so far as to keep it in good working order. But in the case of tyranny, either in the body politic, or in the individual, the sovereign regards immediate gratification only. Hence, a new contingent of Appetence is added to the sovereign element. The tyrant combines the selfishness of the

Democratic sovereign with a selfishness of his own; that is to say, as 27 × 3 = 81, 81 denotes Sovereign Tyranny, aggregate and sole.

But this is not all—The Good of the subject is provided for by the three mixed polities, so far as that good is not inconsistent with, and so far as it ministers to, the aggrandizement of the sovereign; and even a wise Oligarchy will regard the permanent prosperity of its subjects, if not as an end, at least as a means; and the worldly man—its ethical analogue—will in the same way regard his health. But in that state of the individual which Shakespeare also terms tyranny, immediate gratification is the all-absorbing motive. Hence, the notion of the subject-body is converted from that of a permanent into a momentary means of gratification; and, as the notion before was denoted by 3, so now the notion intensified is denoted by the square of 3, 9. And, as the tyrannical sovereign is 27 × 3 = 81, and as the subject is 9, 81 × 9 = 729; consequently, 729 denotes the shortcomings of Tyranny, aggregate and sole. Injustice is represented by that number, and this brings us to the question of negative Ideas.

In the Euthyphron, the Idea of the Unholy is mentioned. Aristotle also objects, that, if there are Ideas, there must be Ideas of negations. The objection is intelligible from Aristotle's point of view, but not from Plato's. Objectively, there can be no negative Idea; but the psychic principle, we have seen, as a noetic compound of The One and the Indefinite, may be to the noetic faculty an Idea. Hence, that state of the psychic principle in which the sensuous Indefinite is maximized, and the noetic faculty wholly obstructed, may be termed an Idea, especially as it is the antithesis of both Justice and Holiness. But in the case of either Injustice, or Impiety, the state is intrinsic solely: the consequences of transgression are confined to the perpetrator; while the consequences of Justice comprehend the accumulated sympathy and love of all rational and moral beings. Hence, all Ideas of negations contain a sensuous element which is wholly wanting both in the Divine Idea, and in the psychic state of the just man after death. But if, with Aristotle, we regard empirical appearance as objective and ultimate, in that case the hypothesis of Ideas sins against the Law of Parcimony, and the Idea of an objective negation is a fair *reductio ad absurdum*.[13] But Plato would never admit the complete objectivity of either the sensible impression, or of its skeletons, Time and Space. The origin of these entities will be considered in the next sub-section.

5. *Evil.*

Plato recognised two modes of causation—efficient and sequential. But the efficient was essential to the commencement of the series of antecedents and consequents. Hence, every series must have had an efficient principle somewhere.

But efficients are of two kinds—the Supreme efficient, God; and the inferior efficient, man. Now, evil consisted in not seeing the Idea, the Supreme efficient. But this imperfection arose from our mistaking the sensuous impression for the ultimate and absolute reality. In our present state we cannot quite unsee sensible things; but by different courses of conduct we can indefinitely increase or diminish the influences of the senses, and proportionally approach or retrocede from the Idea. Hence, the senses are the evil under which we labour; and, as the senses really mean only a set of sequences, the law of antecedence and consequence is the cause of our spiritual blindness. But, as time and space are abstractions of portions of sensible sequences, time and space express in brief all the occasions of moral evil.

The Supreme Efficient is absolutely perfect, without speck or flaw. The Supreme Efficient, therefore, can in no case be held to be the author of evil. Consequently, evil must be imputed to the inferior efficient, man.

But, as man will in certain cases after death be remitted to a purely spiritual state, and as sensible sequences are the thing which is to be accounted for, the origin of sensible sequences must be sought in a state in which they did not actually exist. Hence, the well-known doctrine of Pre-existence.

In a purely spiritual state the psychic principle consists of intuitive power and the higher susceptibilities. But, as the cognitive faculty is intuitive, the cognitive faculty cannot err, and so the blame must rest with the emotive element. In this present state of things, the emotive element is the guiding principle of the ambitious man, who stands midway between the philosopher and the worldly-minded man. Pride, therefore, in some shape or other, appears to have been the original trespass—the only conceivable offence in a purely spiritual state. But, however this may have been, it is certain that Plato regarded the sensuous organism as an undue development of the relative at the expense of the rational element of the psychic principle. In the myth in the Phædrus, the soul is represented as losing its wings, and sinking down to earth in consequence of its collision with other aspiring souls. And in the myth in the Gorgias, the state of the soul after death is said to be determined by the habits which it contracted here. In the tenth book of the Laws, the development of the individual is not, it is alleged, interfered with by the Deity. And these statements, coupled with the mythic doctrine of metempsychosis, would seem to indicate that Plato held in part a theory of the external world similar to that brought into prominence by Brown. And thus the Platonic ethics confirm the views already given of the subjectivity of time and space—of the transient and the *quasi*-permanent.[14]

The religious belief of Plato is a consequence of the same notion—the difference between the two efficients, God and man. The Supreme Efficient manages the objective universe—Himself—according to the dictates of Supreme Intelligence. These dictates cannot, consequently, be altered by any offerings of prayer or of sacrifice on the part of inferior intelligences. Prayer and sacrifice may, when duly regulated, be proper vehicles of public instruction, and may be a proper mode of expressing our subjective feelings. But prayer, as a request, has, according to Plato, no objective efficacy. Man, in proportion to his ethical progress, will attract more and more the Divine sympathy, which he will forfeit by an opposite course of conduct. But the Deity is not wrought into a state of positive and active antipathy. Our misery hereafter will be self-inflicted; and our happiness will also in the first instance depend upon ourselves, but it will be enhanced by the sympathies of all rational and moral beings.[13]

Plato's theory of the origin of evil is not, as has been often alleged, an attempt to shove the difficulty out of sight. It is a necessary consequence of his principles, that where there is a sequence, there must be an efficient; and that the efficient is prior to its sequents, in the order of thought. But the relation between the psychic efficient and the sensuous sequences brings us to Plato's theory of the will.

6. *The Will.*

The vexed question of the freedom of the will does not mar the symmetry of the Platonic ethics. At the same time, it is conceived that Plato's views contain all that is sound in the conflicting modern theories, undisguised by metaphor.

Two *Idola Theatri*—notions out of place—have mainly, if not wholly, caused the prevalent confusion. These *Idola* are the legal notion of freedom in at least two different senses, and the mechanical notion of impulse; and this latter has gradually widened into the more general notion of physical causation.

For the legal metaphor, Plato has himself unwittingly paved the way. The Republic is one long comparison of the individual to the body politic. Plato, besides, describes the soul of the tyrant—the vicious man—as filled with the very essence of slavery. Hence, the comparison of virtue to freedom was natural. But, as will be seen, Plato was not led astray by the metaphor. Strictly speaking, Plato would have denied that either the virtuous or vicious man was free in the common ethical sense of that time.

The significations of the word free which bear on the present question are two. The first denotes the condition of the Slave as opposed to that of the free man. The second denotes mere exemption from penalties, either at the hands of the State, or of the individual.

The term freedom in the first sense connoted the following notions, all of which are excluded from the term servitude. The law looked on the freeman as the ultimate root and source of certain proceedings of which it took cognizance, and which it accordingly imputed to him. The slave, on the other hand, had no *locus standi;* he was held to be the mere conduit of his master's intentions. Even when the slave fell under the power of the state, his master's intention was either expressed or presumed. His master handed him over to the public authority. Freedom, therefore, in this sense, denotes merely the imputability of actions; and the metaphor, so restricted, is harmless enough. But no system of ethics, not even extreme necessitarianism, denies the *ethical* imputability of actions to the agent. What the extreme necessitarian denies is the justice of legal punishment, and not the moral reference of the action to the agent, with its moral consequences of praise and blame.

But freedom has another signification. Every law is really an alternative. Every law says, "Do *or* suffer," "forbear *or* suffer." Now, the sovereign is subject to no alternatives. Every moment of the slave's wretched life is subject to alternatives, either positive or negative, which emanate from his master's caprice. The freeman has, at least, some portion of his time unbroken by positive alternatives. But, as the slave generally obeys the command, and escapes the penalty, extrinsic influence is the prominent portion of the notion slavery. The slave is not as the freeman—he is not free. But free in this sense is quite different from free in the former sense; for the slave may prefer disobedience: in which case he will suffer the penalties of default. But in this sense the slave is morally free. Prometheus, chained to the rock, defies the Autocrat of the universe. Even Omnipotence cannot be conceived as bending the will, save by infusing motives which the reason of the agent adopts as his own.

The two distinct meanings were mixed together in the controversies which arose out of the doctrine of original sin. On the one hand, sin was to be imputed to man; man was, consequently, a source of action, and therefore free. On the other hand, metaphysical hypotheses as to the nature of the Deity excluded even the Promethean choice of obedience or disobedience. Man was, therefore, less *free* in the second sense than the slave; and therefore, according to the first sense, not responsible. The confusion was, and is still, increased by a misconception of mechanical impulse.

A billiard ball, for example, would be considered as totally passive. Yet the weight of the ball is not only an antecedent to the beginning of motion, but also an antecedent which continues to act after the stroke is given. But, as the weight of the ball is constant, while the stroke is variable, the stroke is the only thing to be practically considered. In this way the analogy of impulse is rather against than in favour of the extrinsic necessity of human action. But, as the stroke appears to be the sole agent in the case, the supposed analogy excludes the alternative of freedom in the second sense, and consequently responsibility in the first.

On the other hand, in the case of motion, there is really an analogue to the outward motive. A mouse cannot move a train, but an engine can. Yet still the analogy fails in the most important point; for, to make it complete, the body moved should have a power of refusing to move at all according to circumstances. But, whenever the question of circumstances is raised, the reason must be appealed to. A thousand points of resemblance will not conceal the real diversity of a rational and self-conscious agent and an irrational and unconscious object.

Plato's theory of the will is altogether free from metaphor. The various movements of the body bear to each other the relation of concauses—of antecedents and consequents, as understood by Hume and Brown. This relation Plato terms necessity.[14] But all such series imply, in Plato's opinion, an efficient principle, from which, at least in part, the entire series is evolved. That efficient is the psychic principle—the beginning of all human agency. But it is implied in this that the psychic principle is something more than a beginning. Were the psychic principle a beginning, and nothing but a beginning, it would be a mere antecedent. But as, in Plato's opinion, an antecedent is relative, not only to its consequent, but also to its preceding antecedent, and so on to infinity, to suppose the psychic principle a mere antecedent would be equivalent to accepting the Heracleitan doctrine of flux. There are, therefore, according to Plato, two kinds of causation (if the word must be used), spiritual and sensible: the latter derives all its vitality from the former."

But in neither case, according to Plato, is the notion of freedom applicable. Sensual indulgences— a portion of the sensible sequences—obstruct the faculty of intuition. The opposite course of conduct indefinitely diminishes the obstacles interposed by sensual habits; but in the former case the noetic faculty is totally obstructed. The patient cannot see; for scales have grown upon his eyes. In the latter case, he cannot help seeing; for the scales have been partially removed. They have become so attenuated, that they admit a few struggling rays of light. In the former case, the treatment of the patient must begin from without. And the first step is to make the patient feel the state into which he has sunk. This can only be done by negative logic, as applied to ethical and metaphysical questions. Its subjective effects—internal consistency, and a healthier tone of mind—have been already dwelt on; its objective efficacy remains to be considered.

In conclusion—of the two metaphors, Freedom and Necessity, freedom is the least illusive. If we must choose between the two, the former is the least objectionable. But, it is conceived, all that is really intelligible in the metaphor is, first, that spiritual efficiency and sensible sequence differ in kind; and, second, that all external commands are really alternatives. One spiritual being can influence another only by making him see things in the same light. But in that case both the teacher and pupil, at the end of the lesson, are exactly in the same case; they each see, and cannot help seeing, the same thing in the same light. The metaphors freedom and necessity are only applicable in cases of doubt; and doubt *ex vi termini* implies partial knowledge, and partial ignorance. No one with his eyes sound and open can in the broad day-light see darkness. No one, in Plato's language, can wittingly choose evil as the end and aim of all his being. The fact that men do what they know will be injurious is only an apparent exception to Plato's formula. It is a well-known law, that, when emotion vivifies part of a mental picture, the rest fades away. The temptation is set forth in its most attractive colours, while the restraining force is reduced to a mere intellectual symbol. But the fact that men are restrained by actual remonstrance, or by some accident which brings into relief the rest of the picture, is a *varians in proximo* experiment in favour of Plato's theory of the will. Its complement will be found in Dialectic—the process which partially removes the scale from the mental eye; the object of which, to drop metaphor, is to minimize sensual influences.

7. *Dialectic.*

Objectively, as has been observed, there can be no compromise between existence and nonentity. An objective zero is an absurdity. Until we introduce a reference of some kind, absolute nonentity is unmeaning; and the nature of the reference is the basis of Plato's psychology.

In the perfect state of the psychic principle, never realized in this world, the cognitive or intuitive faculty sees the Idea as it is, face to face. The last stage of psychic degradation is to mistake one of the myriad relations of the Idea for the absolute and ultimate reality. But, as even the philosopher cannot unsee the sensible scheme, the next best thing is to be convinced of its relativity. And to show the relativity of sensible appearances is the function of Dialectic, which is thus an instrument at once of metaphysical investigation and of moral, and of what we now would call religious improvement.

Dialectic has two methods: the sensible method, and the noetic method.[19] The sensible method deals with the relation of the Idea to the sensuous indefinite. The noetic method deals with the relations of objective entities in the order of thought. The sensible method provides us with a provisional solution of the problem before us. The noetic method traces the solution up to the absolute preliminary of all things—to that which is the Beginning of everything, and of which nothing is the beginning.

The sensible method proceeds as follows:—A problem being given, a provisional hypothesis is assumed as a solution of the difficulty. The provisional hypothesis is generally suggested by the crude generalizations of every-day language. Language records empiricism, but is framed on a false assumption—the universality of the fact of sequence. The principle being suggested by common language, the affirmative is assumed to be true; and its fitness is tested by a detailed examination of all cases in which the difficulty occurs. Should the hypothesis fit all the cases, no further positive process is necessary for the present; but the value of the hypothesis may be tested by trying the effect of its negation on the original problem, as well as on other things. The uses of denying a hypothesis are very great; for, even though unanswerable difficulties result from the position of a hypothesis, still greater difficulties may result from its negation. And, according to Plato, the greatest and wisest of men can relatively to all subjects merely choose between two difficulties, and put up with the least. That there must be difficulties, is obvious; for we see the Idea but in part. In all speculative questions, then, the rule must be—of two difficulties, choose the least.

This canon, axiomatic though it be, is nearly always forgotten in practice.[19]

The result thus obtained by positive and negative deduction is as follows :—In a case of doubt, the negative conclusion shows what a thing is not. But the affirmative conclusion has no such virtue; at best it represents but a balance of difficulties. If it is impossible to reject the affirmative position—if its difficulties however, great, are less than those of its negation—we have discovered an Idea or Ideas still in the ore, and thickly entrusted with sensuous deposit.

The Idea thus obtained is but a rough approximation. The real constituents of the Idea are, however, discernible in the empirical formation. But as the Idea—the Definite—results from the combination of The One and The Indefinite, to examine all actual varieties of the kind is the best means of approximating most closely to the Idea. But all actual varieties are, in Plato's opinion, three, and three only; and when we have arranged the three varieties according to the order of thought, and seen how on the one hand they converge towards unity, and on the other diverge towards the Indefinite, we have reached the highest degree of certainty that sensible knowledge admits.[20]

Thus, to take the example given by Plato, that combination of the objective and the subjective, articulate spoken sound, is resolvable into three elements—the vowel, the mute, and the liquid. The vowel and mute are in direct opposition; and the mute presupposes the vowel, but the converse does not hold. The liquid is a vowel so far as it is not a mute, and a mute so far as it is not a vowel. The liquid, therefore, presupposes both vowel and mute in the order of thought. But, as no one variety can be fully known until we know the other two, the three varieties are of necessity connected; and seeing one variety, we see all. Consequently, the knowledge of the two Extremes, and their Indifference, is one and the same. But, seeing all three varieties, we also see that no one variety is ever merged in the other. Hence, the Platonic *dictum*, that every Idea is a Part, but every Part is not an Idea;[21] and we know from the fragment of Xenocrates before referred to, that Plato habitually analyzed life into Ideas and Parts, continuing the process until he reached the five elements in their five figures. Xenocrates in all probability refers to Plato's lectures; at all events, it was Plato's settled view, for Xenocrates uses the imperfect tense.

It has been already observed that with Plato every sensible object is particular. Hence, the three Parts are really groups of individuals. But, to know one Part fully, we must know the other two; and, as each individual may occupy different and even opposite positions in the scale of comparison, that object, which, for example, appears beautiful side by side with some other object, may appear ugly when compared with a third. But since, in collecting the individuals which compose the group, we are engaged in a process of perpetual comparison, the relativity of sensible objects *inter se* can hardly escape our notice. Now, to see the relativity of sensible objects is to be aware of their comparative worthlessness, and to be aware of their worthlessness is the *sine quâ non* of ethical efficiency—of Justice in the Platonic sense. Dialectic, therefore, is the instrument of ethical progress, the steps of which have been already pointed out.

Generalizing the preceding example, we may define the Idea to be the Triune Limitation to which all Higher Existences perfectly, consciously, and spontaneously conform, and to which our subjective tendencies owe their transient actuality. But, as all objects are objects of either mediate or immediate utility, or both—are either ends or means, or both—it follows that all sensible objects with reference to their utilities partake of the Idea of the Beautiful. But, as in the objective sphere there is neither time nor space, that is to say, as God is neither transient nor material—and as the sole differentiating law is the law of thought, and as God is the objective efficient of all utilities mediate or immediate—it follows that the Beautiful is the universal Idea.[23]

In the tenth book of the Republic there is said to be an Idea of a couch. This has been considered either as a proof that Plato's Idea is the modern abstraction, or as a *reductio ad absurdum* of the hypothesis. But, if God be the objective efficient of utilities, and if God be intelligent, He must know that a couch is useful, and may from the human point of view (which He also knows) be beautiful. Further, being intelligent, He must know that indifference of means and end by which a couch or any other object is at the same time most useful and most beautiful. But the indifference of means and ends is an Idea. There is, therefore, an objective Idea of a couch, and this Idea is one; as it is the Divine intuition, which is in immediate relation to its antecedent, the Divine intelligence, and which is not differenced by time or by space."

We may now see the meaning of Aristotle's account of Plato's psychological Numbers. The purely spiritual psychic principle sees the Idea face to face. The noetic faculty looks and sees; it has knowledge at first hand. The number of intuition is, therefore 1. In the highest kind of knowledge given to man, mathematics and physics, so far as they are mathematical, there is a faint tinge of sensuous colour. Hence, 2 is the number of the highest science, that is, intuition, and the sensible indefinite $= 1 + 1 = 2$. In the next step—empirical knowledge—there is knowledge more or less abstract, and reference to fact; that is to say, intuition, abstraction, and reference to fact, $= 1 + 1 + 1 = 3$. And 4 is the number of the most concrete process—the actual sensible impression—as the whole of the preceding process is consciously referred to the bodily organism, that is to say, intuition, abstraction, reference to fact, and reference to organ, $= 1 + 1 + 1 + 1 = 4$. The noetic faculty is, consequently, employed even in sensation, but the vast majority of men never see the significance of the process. To them the noetic faculty is in practical abeyance; it is a slave to the tyrant sense. In Plato's psychology, therefore, as in his ontology, we find $4 + 3 + 2 + 1 = 10$, the maximum of his eidetic numbers.[24]

Before we dismiss the Platonic psychology, it may be observed that, though Plato regards the material of both the modern, primary, and secondary qualities as entirely subjective, he yet concedes greater objectivity to measured than to unmeasured sensations. But this does not show that he was not an idealist in the modern sense of the term. The objective basis of Number is The Idea; and whenever we obtain numerical formulæ, we are, according to him, verging on pure noetic reality.[28]

It will be seen from this brief sketch of Plato's sensible method, how completely his notion of the ultimate object of logic differs from the Aristotelian conception. The Idea is unique both relatively to the subject and to the absolute Deity. Hence, The Idea cannot be given in or through any other Idea. By running " up and down" the scale of sensible things, we see their relativity; and in seeing relativity, we *eo ipso* see reality—the relative implies the absolute. But, as Aristotle's logic is substantially the logic of modern times, the absurdity of seeing in Plato's Idea the modern abstraction in an imaginative dress is apparent.

The noetic method need not detain us long. It is simply intuition according to the order of thought. It may be observed that Plato's law obviates the objection which Sir W. Hamilton, and Mr. Mansel urge against the possibility of knowing the Absolute, viz.: that if the Absolute be a term of the relation knowledge, the Absolute becomes wholly relative. It is apparent that, as the lower steps imply the upper, but not conversely, the absolute may be relative to all terms below it, which is Plato's notion, and absolute from that up: besides, the higher faculty, according to Plato, will not modify or colour the object in the slightest degree. It will know as it is known.

We may now see the full value of negative logic. As an instrument of psychological investigation, it teaches us our ignorance, and clarifies our notions; as an instrument of ethical education, it shows us the relativity of sensations—it removes the scale from our mental eye, and enables it to turn to the light; it conducts the psychic principle to the first step in the noetic ascent, and qualifies it to take its proper position in the hierarchy of Good.

In a much disputed passage towards the end of the

Philebus the hierarchy of Good is delineated as follows:—*First*, all things which deal immediately with the Limit, and in this way participate in the absolute and superessential Good. That is to say, in the order of objectivity, the Idea relatively to its elements stands next to The Good, of which our notion is negative. *Second*, the Beautiful, the Symmetrical, the Complete, the Adequate. That is to say, The Idea considered as the result of combination is logically consequent to The Idea considered relatively to its elements. *Third*, the intuitive faculty and Prudence. That is to say, the psychic principle, as saturated with self-cognition, is at once subject and object, and accordingly logically consequent to The Idea, which is wholly an object. *Fourth*, speculative and practical branches of knowledge, and also professional skill, not consciously grounded on scientific principles. That is to say, these branches contain a purely subjective, as well as a noetic element, and are therefore logically consequent to both the psychic principle— the subject-object—and to The Idea. *And, fifth and last*, pure pleasures; that is to say, the law of antecedence and consequence, so far as it does not obstruct noetic efficiency. If the preceding view of The Idea be sound, the meaning of the passage is clear. The Good constitutes an Idea. The one Extreme is the most objective of objects—The Idea in immediate relation to the superessential, and as yet unknown, Absolute. The other Extreme is the most subjective of objects which can be called Good—sensuous pleasure which does not interfere with noetic efficiency. The Indifference of the two Extremes is the psychic principle, which, being self-cognitive, is both subject and object, and which as noetic power confronts the Idea, and as emotive susceptibility is in contact with pleasure. The second grade of the hierarchy is The Idea, regarded as the result of its elements, and in relation to the subject. And the fourth grade contains a noetic element which has an affinity to the noetic faculty, and an empirical element which savours of the Indefinite. In other words, God and the just man in their mutual relation constitute the Idea of Good, to be more fully realized hereafter.[16]

But, if The Good involves the highest state of the psychic principle Justice, while Injustice is confined to a subordinate and isolated existence,[37] and if the opposite states Justice and Injustice subsume the Platonic psychology, physics, and metaphysics, and if Justice and Injustice are Ideas, though not of coordinate rank, it is submitted that The Idea is in the strictest sense identical with the philosophy of Plato. One Idea still remains to be considered—the relation of the just soul after death to the prime Antecedent.

IX.

IMMORTALITY.

Αὐτὰρ ὁ γυμνώθη ῥακέων πολύμητις.
Hom. *Od.* xxii. 1.

Plato owes nearly all his popular reputation to his advocacy of the immortality of the soul. His arguments on that point are technical, and his authority should not in fairness be cited by any one who is not prepared to embrace his system in its integrity. His argument is a case of the antithesis which, he alleges, exists between noetic and sensible objects.

The bodily organism is a portion of the sensible Indefinite. In strictness, the body denotes the sum of cerebral sequences with which we find ourselves bound up. Death, as an antecedent, is another sequence, which, meeting the cerebral, brings it to an end; and the result of the meeting of the two sequences is a new phenomenon—the corpse.'

We have seen that sensible sequences are made up of a temporal and a non-temporal element; and that time, a portion only of the law of antecedence and consequence, does not affect that which is non-temporal—that which in positive language is eternal.

Death is temporal. Death, therefore, does not reach the noetic portion of the psychic principle—intuitive power, and the higher susceptibilities.

This argument is reproduced in various shapes, which are in reality the same at bottom. Thus, the doctrine of Recollection which is found in the Meno, the Phædo, and the Phædrus, means that sensible sequences presuppose a noetic basis in the order of thought. The two notions, temporal and non-temporal existence, being correlated, the logical and substantive independence of the latter, and the consequent logical and substantive dependence of the former, are at once apparent. But, to pass from a consequent to its antecedent is, in the language of the understanding, a mode of recollection. The doctrine of Pre-existence is another name of the same thing.[1]

The same argument—the antithesis of the noetic and the sensible—appears in the Phædrus in the shape that the soul is eternal, because it is the Principle of Motion. Motion is sequence; and sequence is the law of phenomena, which implies, as before, a non-temporal or eternal element.[2]

In the end of the Phædo, the stress of the argument rests on the objective qualities of The Idea. The Idea is not objectively bound by the law of antecedence and consequence; and, as Like is known by Like, the noetic subject sees that it resembles its noetic object. It sees itself to be non-temporal, and therefore not subject to the sensible process of growth and decay The soul, therefore, intuitively sees that it is not affected by anything which brings in its train the phenomenon Death.[4]

The argument from Recollection appeals to psychic fact, the logical relation of the sensible and the noetic; the argument from the Principle of Motion appeals partly to psychic fact, and partly to objective noetic relation; and the argument from the nature of The Idea appeals mainly to objective reality. The three arguments are in reality the same, although our attention in each case is directed from different points of view.

In the Republic, the subject is treated of from the ethical point of view. Vice is the worst possible state of the soul; but vice is the bodily influence maximized, which merely obstructs the noetic faculty. Vice does not destroy the psychic principle; therefore, nothing will. There is no analogue to Death or obstruction in the noetic sphere. No spiritual being can injure any one but himself. The ethical view, as usual in Plato, verges on the metaphysical. The same argument occurs in the Phædo, in the form that the soul is not a harmony—a result of organization.[5]

Various arguments in the Phædo, which appear at first sight to be arguments *ad hominem*, are really grounded on the same antithesis. Thus, the soul is not the result of organization; it is not, for example, like the sound of a lyre. For the antithesis of sound is the perpetual silence of the instrument, that is, its disruption. But, virtue being the highest state of the soul, vice by parity of reasoning ought to destroy the soul. But, as there is an indefinite progress in vice, as well as in virtue, vice is certainly not the analogue of the disruption of the instrument; and, as there is nothing in death to make men less unjust—or, in modern language, less vicious and sinful—Death, which *ex hypothesi* is wholly phenomenal, cannot touch that which is non-phenomenal; that is, the noetic is the perfect antithesis of the sensible.⁶

The same antithesis is found in the argument that the soul opposes the body. The psychic principle is the efficient of motion—all movements are merely concausal. That is, as before, the noetic is the antithesis of the sensible.⁷

The argument that Contraries come into being out of Contraries is, in the first instance (like St. Paul's illustration of the seed), an *ad hominem* reply to a sensualist.⁸ The soul is mortal, for life is followed by death; growth merges in decay; and this is the universal law of all things. True, Plato replies; growth merges in decay, but decay not the less eventuates in growth. Therefore, even according to what the sensualist holds to be the ultimate and universal law, the psychic principle *may* be revivified after death. But the argument means something more; it means, as was before shown, that the notion antecedence and consequence involves a noetic element; and, consequently, the sensible phenomenon—the dead body—so far from proving the mortality of the soul, in reality proves the very reverse. Every phe-

nomenon presupposes a non-phenomenal element.
The same argument, of course, may be extended to
the cases of sleep and intoxication, which seem to
favour the sensual hypothesis. The antithesis is as
before.*

Plato's doctrine, that we have an intuition of the
Ego, answers a practical objection to the doctrine of
immortality, which is this:—Every one believes that
there was a time in which he was not alive; consequently, a time may come from which also he will be
absent. Generalizing this, it must be admitted that,
if Time pervade the entire of the psychic principle—
if our whole and inmost being is a series of antecedents and consequents—then it must be allowed that
all analogy teaches the final natural mortality of the
conscious agent. But, if we have an intuition of
non-temporal existence—if we see that the law of
antecedence and consequence merely expresses a part
of our psychic experiences—then all analogies which
are cases of that law, in reality, on Plato's showing,
are evidence in favour of the spirituality of the soul.
Now, the *fact* that the psychic principle is more than
a series, is, after Berkeley, admitted in the present
day by Mr. Mill and Mr. Mansel. Mr. Mill, certainly,
will not be accused of mysticism, and Mr. Mansel is
pledged to Sir W. Hamilton's philosophy of common
sense. Their testimony is, consequently, unex-
ceptionable. Of English Metaphysicians, at least,
Berkeley, Mr. Mill, and Mr. Mansel concede Plato's
first principle—the intuition of a non-temporal

Ego, as opposed to the concomitant series of bodily changes; and thus we meet the Platonic antithesis in a modern shape.[10]

But the objection derived from the absence of sentient existence *a parte ante* can in fairness only be used by those who maintain the universality of Time—who hold that time reaches the depths of the psychic principle. On any other hypothesis, the objection is unintelligible,

> "For, Memory dealing but with Time,
> And he with Matter, can she climb
> Beyond her own material prime?"

Every argument used by Plato, then, is grounded on the antithesis between the Noetic and the Sensible. The localization of the triple soul in the Timæus will present no difficulty to any one who will recollect the symbolism of the Dialogue—the most Ultra-spiritualist might hold the brain to be the organ of thought.[11]

The relation of the psychic principle to the Deity is purely spiritual. The Deity is the self-sustained Antecedent, Who sustains the dependent psychic consequent in the order of thought. But, again, we must recollect, that noetic existence is not a mere logical schematism. Emotive susceptibility is inseparable from cognitive power in the psychic compound. Consequently, the individuality of the psychic principle is not merged in the Divine Antecedent; the lustre of no star is ever lost in the brightness of the sun of the noetic system."[12] The relation of the purely spiritual soul to its Antecedent will constitute an Idea of the highest type. The one Extreme is The Object—the Deity, absolutely good, and absolutely known as He is. The other Extreme is the Subject, knowing as it is known. And the Indifference of the two unmodified Extremes is the Subject united to The Object by the bonds of knowledge and of sympathy. But the full glories of the final state will not be seen until the Soul, after many a wanderering, shall stand, stripped of all disguise, in native majesty on the threshold of the long-sought Home.

NOTES.

I. Note¹, p. 7.—The preceding Essay does not necessarily postulate any special arrangement of the Platonic writings; in brief, it asserts that the negative logic of Plato is the first and only step to the doctrine of The Idea. But, as this statement is implicitly at variance with Mr. Grote's two propositions (*vide* Preface, pp. ix, x), this is perhaps a proper place to consider his opinions in general.

If the views advocated in the Essay be sound, there is, strictly speaking, no organon of the positive side of Plato's philosophy. The positive faculty acts intuitively (Rep. vii. 518, C.–E.; Phædr. 249, E.); it therefore sees things as they are (Crat. 386, E.); but, as Plato held that sensation was subject to the Heracleitan law of flux (Arist. Metaphys., A. 6; M. 4), there is, it is conceived, no necessary inconsistency in positing two kinds of knowledge—noetic and sensible. And Protagoras having laid down that in *all* cases of cognition the subject was modified and altered by the object (Theæt. 152, A; 160, D.; Crat. 385, E.; 386, C.), the first step was to attempt to prove that there is absolute knowledge—meaning, not knowledge without a subject—in Mr. Grote's terms, a *cognitum* without a *cognoscens* (which, of course, is unmeaning)—but a state wherein the *cognoscens* and the *cognitum* remain mutually unaltered. That there cannot be a *cognoscens* without a *cognitum*, Plato admits, Charm. 167, B.–168, B.; but he would maintain that there may be a *cognitum* without a *cognoscens;* although not, of course, existing in that special relation; that is, in Plato's opinion things logically and substantively connected are not, in the strict sense, necessarily correlatives, Arist. Met., Δ. 11; *cf.* Mill's Hamilton, pp. 42, 92, 1st ed. If the distinction of modified and unmodified cognition, be kept in view, all

Mr. Grote's charges of Plato's inconsistency in admitting at one time, and denying at another, the relativity of knowledge, fall to the ground; see especially Mr. Grote's remarks on the Phædrus, cited below. Of course, as the Essay professes merely to state Plato's views *ex parte*, it would be quite out of place to discuss the possibility of absolute knowledge. As to the various meanings of relative knowledge, see Mr. Mill's Hamilton, cap. II. That, as a matter of fact, Plato did hold the doctrine of unmodified knowledge, *vid.* Phæd. 65, E.; 66, B. D.-67, A. B.; 78, D.; 79, D.; 80, B.; Crat. 386, E.; Soph. 248, A.; Sym. 211, A.-B.; Phædr. 247, D. E.; Tim. 51, D.-52, D.; Epist. vii. 343, E.

The contradictions which, in Mr. Grote's opinion, exist between certain dialogues will be considered, as each topic arises. But one general remark may be made here. Mr. Grote seems to think that Plato regarded his positive philosophy as a complete solution of the difficulties raised by negative discussion. But this is not the case: Plato always sets forth his positive theory as an approximation merely—as the least of two difficulties; as more intelligible than the sensualism of Heracleitus, or the unity of Parmenides. Man, as long as he is connected with a sensuous organism, cannot know things adequately, Phæd. 66, D; 85, C.-D.; 100, A.; 107, A. B.; Rep. vi. 505, A.; 506, E.; Rep. vii. 517, B. C.; Leg. x. 897, D. E.; Epin. 980, A.; Phædr. 246, A.; 248, A.; Epist. ii. 312, E.-313, A.; Tim. 29, B.-D. With regard to εἰκότες λόγοι, see the definition of εἰκών, Crat. 432, A. B, and its difference from number. The passage in the Phæd. 92, D., which Mr. Grote (iii. p. 246, n.) contrasts with the usage of εἰκότες λόγοι in the Timæus, is in reality in strict conformity with it, and with another passage, Phæd. 100, A. The sun is the physical analogue of The Good, Rep. vi. 509, B.; vii. 517, B.-C. We are forced to view the former through a medium, Phæd. 99, D.; the same illustration occurs, Rep. 516, B; Leg. x. D.-E.; *cf.* Phædr. 250, B.); εἰκόνες and εἰκότες λόγοι are therefore the media between pure noetic reality and the unmodified noetic faculty; that is, the analogical concrete narratives—the spiritual translated into the sensuous—the verbal duplicates of εἰκασία, the lowest mental process: Rep. vi. 511, E.

Plato's notion, that our highest degree of knowledge is seeing but in part, explains what Mr. Grote considers a marked contradiction between Plato's conception of absolute knowledge and Plato's conformity to individuals and occasions. Mr. Grote's objections are so consistently urged, that a single extract will be sufficient:—

"Plato is usually extolled by his admirers, as the champion of the Absolute—of unchangeable forms, immutable truth, objective necessity cogent and binding on every one. He is praised for having refuted Protagoras; who can find no standard beyond the individual recognition and belief, of his own mind or that of some one else. There is no doubt that Plato often talks in that strain: but the method followed in his dialogues, and the general principle of method which he lays down, here as well as elsewhere, point to a directly opposite conclusion. Of this the Phædrus is a signal instance. Instead of the extreme of generality, it proclaims the extreme of specialty. The objection which the Socrates of the Phædrus advances against the didactic efficacy of written discourse is founded on the fact, that it is the same to all readers—that it takes no cognizance of the differences of individual minds, nor of the same mind at different times. Socrates claims for dialectic debate the valuable privilege, that it is constant action and reaction between two individual minds—an appeal by the inherent force and actual condition of each to the like elements in the other—an ever-shifting presentation of the same topics, accommodated to the measure of intelligence and cast of emotion in the talkers, and at the moment. The individuality of each mind—both of questioner and respondent—is here kept in view as the governing condition of the process. No two minds can be approached by the same road, or by the same interrogation. The questioner cannot advance a step except by the admission of the respondent. Every respondent is the measure to himself. He answers suitably to his own belief; he defends by his own suggestions; he yields to the pressure of contradiction and inconsistency, *when he feels them*, and not before. Each dialogist is (to use the Protagorean phrase) the measure to himself of truth and falsehood, according as he himself believes it. Assent or dissent, whichever it may be, springs only from the free working of the individual mind, in its actual condition then and there. It is to the individual mind alone that appeal is made, and this is what Protagoras asks for."—Vol. ii., p. 261.

But the specializing adaptation of Plato to individuals and occasions—his being all things to all men—relates to negative logic only. To join two Platonic metaphors, every human being labours more or less under obstructed vision; the treatment, therefore, varies with each case, and some cases are hopeless—the most skilful practitioner gives them up in despair, Theæt., 150, D.-E., cf. Theag. 130, E.-131, A.; and in no case can the physician guarantee complete success. Were the obstruction completely removed, the mental eye would see The Idea face to face. To drop metaphor, Plato's meaning is:—We have here sensible or empirical knowledge; but sensible knowledge is essentially mediate; Theæt. 184, B. C.; 1, Alc. 129, E.; and to recognise its mediacy is the first step towards immediate knowledge—which, no man here ever completely attains to. To prove, then, the mediacy or essential and inherent relativity of sensible knowledge is the task of negative Dialectic, Epist. vii. 343, D., and the *modus operandi* must vary with the individual and occasion. There is, therefore, it is submitted, not only no contradiction, but complete conformity, between the two sides of Plato's philosophy. The negative operation—which varies in each case—can only remove a layer of the cataract; and the better light which the patient then discerns is perceived by the inherent and unimpaired, but still materially obstructed, power of the eye. The analogy, of course, is mere metaphor, as will be shown in the note on the word Ἰδέα, p. 146. Besides, Plato qualifies the doctrine of Protagoras by the restriction ἂν μὴ φρόνιμός τις ᾖ, Theæt. 183, C.; cf. Leg. iv. 716, C.; ὁ δὴ Θεὸς ἡμῖν πάντων χρημάτων μέτρον ἂν εἴη μάλιστα, πολὺ μᾶλλον ἤ πού τις, ὥς φασιν, ἄνθρωπος. This is what the writer has endeavoured to work out in the section Justice, for φρόνησις is the correlate of Θεός.

SECTION II.

Note ¹, p. 8.—Sensation is the material of δόξα, and is supplied on birth; Theæt. 186, C. Δόξα may be true or false. If true, its practical uses are as valuable as those of ἐπιστήμη, save that the former, as mere empirical fact, cannot be depended on in all cases.—Men. 97, D. E.; 98, A; 99, A. The test of ὀρθὴ δόξα is its power of modifying the future.—Crat. 367, A.-B. The passage generally cited from Phæd. 65, B., merely asserts that sight and hearing are neither accurate nor clear (ἀκριβεῖν μητὲ σαφῶς), which means that they do not convey the highest kind of knowledge. Sight is the paramount sense, Rep. vi. 507, C.; Phædr. 250, D. Then, hearing, cf. Phil. 51, D.-E. As to the provinces of Sense and Reason in perception, vid. Rep. vii. 523, D.-E.; cf. Rep. x. 603, A.

Note ², (ib.).—Phæd. 66, C.; Rep. ix. 580, E.

Note ³, (ib.).—Crat. 411, C.; 436, E.; 439, C.

Note ⁴, p. 9.—Three theories of the representative faculties are discussed by Plato, viz.—(1) mechanical retention; (2) semimechanical suggestion; and (3) his own view, that it is a case of the general physical law of sequence: (1) Theæt. 191, C.; (2) Theæt. 197, B.; (3) Symp. 208, A. B. As to the appropriateness of Sir W. Hamilton's terms, vide note ³⁰, on p. 28.

Note ⁵ (ib.), vide n. ⁷¹, p. 26.

Note ⁶, p. 13.—Theæt. 154, A.; 155, E.; 159, C. D. 161, C.

Note ⁷ (ib.).—Hamilton's Reid, p. 863, n. a. b.; Abbott's "Sight and Touch," p. 76, n. This latter book is a vigorous effort to rehabilitate common sense, and contains a large number of facts and experiments relating to the antecedents of perception; but it is obvious that Mr. Abbott notices the laws of *mechanical* association only, and quite ignores the heteropathic products of the same process. Mr. Abbott's argument is—the completed phenomenon is neither in this nor in that special antecedent singly; it is, therefore, not the result of all of them together. But what the other side insists on is "*connexa valent.*" The subject, however, cannot be discussed in a note: on the other side, *vide* Mill's Ham., caps. IX., XIII, XIV.

Note [8], p. 14.—As to the antecedents, *vid.* Theæt. 184, C.; *cf. ib.* D.; 185, D.-E.; 156, E.-157, A.; 160, B.; 182, B.; 1. Alc. 129, B.-130, A.

Note [9] (*ib.*).—Dreaming and delirium are cited by Socrates, Theæt. 157, E.-158, A.-E., as *ad absurda* of Common Sense: *vid.* note, p. 167.

Note [10] (*ib.*).—Theæt. 153, D. E.; 154, B.

Note [11], p. 15.—Charm. 167, C. D.; *cf.* James Mills, *ap.* Mill's Ham. p. 115.

Note [12] (*ib.*).—Phæd. 60, B. C.; 71, A. B. C.; Theæt. 152, D. E.; 157, A. B. C.; Leg. x. 893, C.-894, A.; Symp. 207, D.-208, A.

Note [13], p. 16.—*Vide* the Myth in the Politicus, 268, E. *et sq.*; and its explanation in the text, pp. 106, 107.

Note [14], p. 17.—Theæt. 182, A.; Leg. x. 893, E.

Note [15] (*ib.*).—Theæt. 186, D. E.; Parm. 166, B. C.

Note [16], p. 18.—Parm. *ib.*

Note [17] (*ib.*).—Parmenides combats the notion that noetic existence depends on the concipient subject, Parm. 132, B. C.; see text, pp. 49, 50; and this theory is the second form of the hypothesis discussed in Theæt. 187, B.-200, D.

Note [18], p. 17.—Theæt. 185, A.

Note [19], *ib.*—Κήρινον ἐκμαγεῖον, Theæt. 191, C.; περιστερεών, 197, D.

Note [20], p. 18—Theæt. 190, C.; 200, B.; *vid.* Mill's Ham. pp. 347-8, 352-3, 1st Ed.

Note [21], p. 19.—Theæt. 195, D.-196, B.

Note [22], p. 20.—Rep.-vi. 510, C.-D.

Note [23] (*ib*).—Rep. vii. 616, C.-D.

Note [24], p. 21.—The test of a genuine induction, according to Mr. Mill, is its efficacy in predicting the future, Logic, III. cap. 2; and, according to Mr. G. H. Lewes, Verification is the criterion which distinguishes modern science from ancient speculation. (Aristotle, p. 69). It is plain that prediction and Verification both waive the questions, What is sensation? Is it the sum of human knowledge?

Note ⁲⁶, p. 21.—Parm. 130, C.; mud or clay is defined as "Earth mixed with Liquid;" that is, the combination of two extremes, Theæt. 147, C. Plato's habit of making use of illustrations taken from things which are considered common, (cf. Soph. 218, D.; Polit. 266, D.; Hip. Maj. 288, D.;) is connected with his view that Divine supervision is exercised in the minutest way, Leg. x. 900, C.; 902, E.

Note, ²⁵ (ib.).—Vide text, p. 74.; Sect. Participation, cf. Theæt. 156, E.; 160, B. Even in Plato's day, to hold solidity to be the objective criterion, was set down as τῶν ἀμυήτων. Dr. Johnson's argument was known: σκληρούς γε λέγεις καὶ ἀντιτύπους ἀνθρώπους. ΣΩ. 'Εισὶ γὰρ ὦ ποῖ, μάλ' εὖ ἄμουσοι. Theæt. 155, E.-156., A.; Soph. 246, A.; Epin. 981, D.

Note ²⁷, p. 22.—Bacon's wishes to confine sense to observation of the experiment. N. Org. I. L., De Aug., v. c. 2.

Note ²⁸, (ib.).—Phædr. 265, D.

Note ²⁹, p. 23.—Crat. 423, B.; as to change, vide ib., 414. C.

Note ³⁰, (ib.).—Crat. 411, D. C.; 436, E.

Note ³¹, p. 24.—Theæt. 201, E.; 203, E.; 206, D.; Crat. 385, B. C.

Note ³², (ib.)—Crat. 436, B.

Note ³³. p. 25.—Theæt. 206, D.-E.

Note ³⁴, (ib.).—Theæt. 206, E.-207, A.

Note ³⁵, (ib).—Theæt. 208, C. As to the defect common to the three varieties, vid. Theæt. 206, E.; 207, D.; 209, E. The arrangement of the varieties of each form of the hypothesis has been taken from the conclusion of the Theætetus. It would, perhaps, have been better to have adhered to the logical order, and have in each case placed the two extremes before their compromise. The arrangement in the conclusion of the Theætetus may have arisen from a wish to close the dialogue with a discussion of the most important variety of the hypothesis.

Note ³⁶, (ib.).—Theæt. 208, C.; Brown cites Mrs. Quickly's speech, Hen. IV. Part 2, Act II. s. i.; as an example of vulgar,

as opposed to scientific suggestion, the ἑκατὸν δέ τε δούραθ'
ἁμάξης.

Note ³¹, p. 26.—The mental operations are, φαντασία, δόξα, and
διάνοια, i. e., the apprehension, judgment, and reasoning of the
common logic. Their verbal counterparts are expressed by λόγοι,
combinations of nouns and verbs. The function of each set is,
affirmation and negation, φάσις καὶ ἀπόφασις, Soph. 263, D.; cf.
ib., 261, E.; Theæt. 202, B.; Leg. x., 895, D.-E.; Epist. vii.,
343, D.; and Mr. Mill's Hamilton, p. 328–9.

Note ³², p. 27.—Theæt. 189, A.; Soph. 263, Δ.-B.; Crat. 388,
B. C.; 409, C.

Note ³³, p. 28.—Soph. 263, A. B.; E. 264, A. B.; Pol. 264, C.;
πίστις is the counterpart of δόξα, Tim. 51, E.; cf. Rep. vi. 511. E.
Φαντασία differs from δόξα, as a presentation differs from its representation, as the latter is in the psychic principle καθ' αὑτήν, and
φαντασία comes δι' αἰσθήσεων, Soph. 264, A. Φαντασία is the ultimate contact of the psychic principle and the body—the sum
of sensible sequences, Phæd. 79, C.; cf. ib., 83, D., the phrase
ἅπερ ἂν τὸ σῶμα φῇ with the φάσις and the ἀπόφασις of the
Sophistes, 263, E.

Note ³⁴, (ib.).—Every verbal description belongs to the class
εἰκόνες, Crat. 432, B.; and all εἰκόνες partake less of ἀληθεία
than the things which they typify, Rep. vi. 511, E. cf. ib. 509, E.-
-510, A.B.; with regard to the two next paragraphs, for Plato's
view of Space, vide Essay, pp. 79–81, and notes; and for Plato's
psychology, see p. 147, 148, and notes.

Note ³⁵, p. 29.—There are three ποιηταί, viz., θεός, δημιουργός,
and μιμητής, Rep. x. 597, B. D. E.; cf. ib., 601, D. The μιμητής
produces φαντάσματα and not ὄντα, 599, A., and cf. ἡ μιμητική,
ib. 603, A. B. The painter represents things as they are presented
to sight, and not as per measure, Rep. 598, A.; cf. 602, D.;
Soph. 235, D.-236, A.; while the poet deals with words, which as
εἰκόνες are the least real objects of the lower faculties, Rep. xi.
544, E. Zeuxis is mentioned twice, Gorg. 453, C. D.

Note ³⁶, p. 30.—Theæt. 210, C.

Note ³⁷, (ib.)—Theæt. 210, C. This is, perhaps, the proper

place to consider a point in which Mr. Grote lays great stress. He specially singles out for attack Plato's doctrine of the Non-Ens, as laid down in the Sophistes, and alleges its inconsistency with Theæt. 188, 189; Euthyd. 284, B. C.; Rep. v. 477, 478; Parm. 160, C.; 163, C. vol. II. 455. But if the distinction between the respective objects of Knowledge and Opinion be recollected, the contradiction vanishes. Objectively, there is either existence, or there is not, Rep. v. 477, A.; and so far Plato assents to Parmenides. Even Mr. Mill concedes the predicate existent or non-existent to Noumena, Ham., pp. 86, 7. But, unless there be a possibility of subjective *non*-existence, Soph. 241. D.; *cf. ib.*, 237, A., 240, E., Plato would accept the doctrine of either Parmenides or Heracleitus. The passages in the Theætetus and the Euthydemus referred to by Mr. Grote are levelled against the Heracleitan exclusiveness; and the second and third propositions in the Parmenides, 142, B.-157, A., are, it is conceived, intended to show the possibility of the Non-Ens. Plato, as stated in the text, lays down that a proposition has two affections—its internal composition, and its extrinsic reference to matter of fact, Soph. 263, A. B.; E. 264, A., B.; Politic. 264, C. (πέπυσαι γοῦν καὶ πιστεύεις εἶναι); Tim. 51, E.; Rep. vi. 511, E.; and the discussion of Theætetus' second definition, Theæt. 187, B.-200, D. In brief, πίστις, or reference to fact, is an essential part of the true proposition, whether mental or verbal (*cf.* Mr. Mill's Ham., pp. 253-4). This, however, is no concession to the common-sense doctrine, Theæt. 158, D. Gorg. 475, E.-476, A.; Lach. 184, E.; and *cf.* the well known Platonic distinction between science and empiricism—; a distinction which at least shows Plato's peculiar views, Arist. Metaph. A. I.

Mr. Grote's objection (II. 452), that Plato's doctrine destroys the universality of the Principle of Contradiction, is another example of the same confusion of the different senses of Non-Ens. The Principle of Contradiction asserts that the same predicate cannot be affirmed and denied of the same subject, in the *same* sense. This Plato admits: objectively, there is either existence, or there is not; objectively, no one idea can encroach on the prerogative of another. Subjectively, there is either reality, or not. The concept, a twenty-legged horse, is subjectively true; it is conceived as having twenty legs. But this does not affect the soundness of Plato's opinion, that we may predicate Existence in different senses. The proposition that vehicles are drawn by twenty-legged horses is, waiving all ethical questions, subjectively true, as soon as it is conceived or enunciated; and the logical affection falsity cannot attach until we refer the proposition to something, either subjective or objective; taking objective either in the sense of the empiricist or Platonist. There cannot be a relation without two things, or at least the same thing viewed as two. It is therefore, it is submitted, no violation of Contradiction to assert that "the non-Existent," in the Platonic sense, "is and is not;" but not, of course, in the same sense, *vid.* Rep. v. 477, A., εἰ δὲ δή τι οὕτως ἔχει, ὡς εἶναί τε καὶ μὴ εἶναι, κ.τ.λ., *cf.* Theæt. 191, A.; οὐ φήσω ἡμᾶς ὀρθῶς ὁμολογῆσαι, ἡνίκα ὡμολογήσαμεν, ἅ τις οἶδει, ἀδύνατον δοξάσαι ἃ μὴ οἶδεν εἶναι αὐτά, καὶ ψευσθῆναι ἀλλά πη δύνατον. Also Soph. τὸ μὴ ὂν, ὧν ἐστι κατά τι, καὶ τὸ ὂν—ὂν οὐκ ἔστι πη. 241, D.; *cf.* Rep. II. 382, B._C. That is, error is a subjective fact, while to the person in error the objective does not exist.

Mr. Grote also objects that Plato's doctrine excludes the pure negative, which simply nullifies belief. But is this so? Can that which nullifies belief be a simple negative? It is quite true that a process of negative argument substitutes nothing in the place of the opinion it demolishes; but then the negative battery must be directed from some determinate point. Even to show that a square circle is a contradiction, postulates, first, that there is, in some way or other, such things, or facts, or suppositions, as are generally called squares or circles; second, that these differ; and that, consequently, to assert that a circle is square is at least unmeaning. Plato's doctrine, it is conceived, provides for the pure negation, which Mr. Grote's does not. He who simply denies, in reality appeals to either the general expeence of all men, or makes an *ad hominem* appeal to the special experience of the believer. Even the sceptic appeals to the admitted fact, that much may be said on both sides of every speculative question. A nullifying process can only dispossess pre-existing belief by calling in the aid of other beliefs, either general or special. A positive quantity cannot be reduced to zero by subtracting zero.

SECTION III.

Note ¹, p. 34.—Theæt. 185, A.-E.

Note ², p 35.—Theæt. 184, E.-185, A.; *cf.* Mill's Logic, III., cap. xiv. on Empirical Laws.

Note ³, (*ib.*).—Rep. vii. 523, E.-524, A.; *cf.* Phæd. 96, E.-97, A.-B.; that is, addition produces the effect of division, and *vice versa.* Also Phæd. 102, B. D.; and Theæt. 154, C.; 155, C.; Hip. Maj. 289, B.-C.; Rep. v. 479, A.; Phæd. 74, B.; for the illustration, see Rep. vii. 523, C.-D.

Note ⁴, p. 36.—*Vide* references in preceding note, and *cf.* the references on n. ⁵.

Note ⁵, p. 37.—Phil. 15, D.

Note ⁶, p. 38.—Phil. 24, C.-25, B.—Cf. the two kinds of measurement πρὸς τοὐναντίον, καὶ πρὸς τὸ μέτριον, &c. The first kind comprehends the ordinary measurements of one sensation by another, either for common sense or scientific purposes; the latter refers to the Idea, πάνθ᾽ ὁπόσα εἰς τὸ μέσον ἀπωκίσθη τῶν ἐσχάτων, Polit. 284, E.

Note ⁷, p. 39.—Charm. 168, B. C. D.

Note ⁸, p. 40.—τὸ πέρας = πᾶν ὅ τί περ ἂν πρὸς ἀριθμὸν ἀριθμὸς ἢ μέτρον ᾖ πρὸς μέτρον, Phil. 25, A.-B.

Note ⁹. p. 41.—περὶ ἕκαστον ἄρα τῶν εἰδῶν πολὺ μέν ἐστι τὸ ὄν, ἄπειρον δὲ πλήθει τὸ μὴ ὄν, Soph. 256, E.; and *cf.* the fourth and fifth propositions of the Parmenides; the former of which shows that τἄλλα in relation to The One is both definite and indefinite, 158, D.-E.; and the latter, that τἄλλα out of all relation to The One admits no predicate whatever, *ib.* 160, A.-B.

N

Note [10], p. 41.—Τὸ ἓ' ἄπειρον ἐκ μεγάλου καὶ μικροῦ τοῦτ' ἴσιον. Met. A. 6.; cf. Phys. iii. 4.3. Aristotle objects that Plato having postulated two indefinites, the Great and the Small, does not make use of them, Phys. iii. 6, 6; but the objection is fully provided for by the propositions of the Parmenides, cited *supra*. The Indefinite is, in fact, a logical antecedent, which cannot be construed to thought as indefinite. If construed, it becomes definite, i. e. positive, τὸ μέγα καὶ τὸ μικρον; Plato uses these terms, Rep. vii. 524, C.

Note [11] (ib.).—Mathematics are hypothetic, Rep. vi. 510, C.; and next to the noetic, that is, dianoetic, ib. 511, C. D. They are the mean between δόξα and νοῦν, ib. D.; cf. Arist. Metaph. A. (i.), 6; ib. N. (xiv.), 3; ib. 6.

Note [12], p. 42.—We may proceed from the Indefinite to the Limit, and *vice versâ*, Phil. 16, A-B., in order to discover the Idea; and therefore, it is conceived, we may describe the Idea according to either method.

Note [13] (ib.).—*Vid.* note 8.

Note [14] (ib.).—Charm. 167, C.-168, B., is an *enumeratio simplex* of faculties and their objects; and the fifth proposition of the Parmenides shows that the indefinite *per se* is incogitable.

SECTION IV.

Note [1], p. 45.—*Vid.* note [14], p. 42. As to the function of the brain, *vid.* Phæd. 96, B. It must be recollected that Plato considered the Heracleitan theory as insufficient, but not false; and its necessary complement is The Idea, Arist. M. (xiii.) 4. The brain was, therefore, a concause. *Vid.* n. [10], p. 167.

Note [2], p. 46.—*Vid.* text, pp. 77-81, and notes.

Note [3] (ib.).—Rep. vi. 490, B.; Tim. 45, C.-D.; Arist. de Anima, i. 2, 8. That the law is a mere statement of fact, and not a condition which precedes and explains the fact of cognition, is plain. Plato held the Heracleitan doctrine of flux; he also held that we have in part intuitive knowledge; see references, note [1], p. 160; and intuition is final, meaning by intuition knowledge without *media* or proof.

Note ¹, p. 49.— *Vid.* note *, p. 40.
Note ², p. 50.—Parm. 132, C.
Note ³ (*ib.*).—Parm. 132, C. This question in the Parmenides is analogous to the modern question of the reality of the external world. The common sense view embodies the mere fact that *all* our perceptions do not depend upon the will, *cf.* Des Cartes:—"Quamvis ideæ illæ a voluntate meâ non pendeant, non ideo constat ipsas a rebus extra me positis necessario procedere," Med. III. Now, it is conceived, Plato's argument is conclusive against all theories of latent mental modifications. They either are in the field of consciousness, or they are not. In the latter case they are extra-mental, *cf.* Mill's Hamilton, p. 285-7. On the other hand, Plato's intuition of the Ego gives us, as its correlative, but not co-ordinate, a knowledge of a *Non-Ego; vid.* section " Immortality," p. 152. Plato's view of the objectivity of the Idea—the principle of number and quantity—is illustrated by a passage in Aristotle—'Ο ἐδ χρόνος ἀριθμός ἐστιν, οὐχ ᾧ ἀριθμοῦμεν, ἀλλ' ὁ ἀριθμούμενος, Phys. IV. 12, 3.

SECTION V.

Note ¹, p. 55.— 'Ιάδες ἐδ καὶ Σικελαί τινες ὕστερον Μοῦσαι ξυννενοήκασιν, ὅτι συμπλέκειν ἀσφαλέστατον ἀμφότερα καὶ λέγειν, ὡς τὸ ὂν πολλά τε καὶ ἕν ἐστιν, ἔχθρᾳ δὲ καὶ φιλίᾳ συνέχεται, Soph. 242, D. E. Plato mentions two varieties of the Pluralists, *ib.* D.; but, as he himself adopted in part the view of Heracleitus, the text has been shaped accordingly, *cf.* Theæt. 152, E. As to his obligations to Pythagoras, Aristotle says that μέθεξις was the Pythagorean μίμησις, Metaph. A. (1.), 6. But see Section Participation, and notes.

Note ², p. 56.—Soph. 251, D.-252, A. The same argument is also fatal to indefinite Flux, *ib.; cf.* Parm. 1st Prop., 137, C.-142, E.

Note ³, p. 57.—Parm. 128, D.; 135, B.C.—Καὶ ἐνὶ λόγῳ—εἰ μέλλεις τελέως γυμνασάμενος εὑρίσκειν διόψεσθαι τὸ ἀληθές. *cf.* ἄνευ γὰρ ἑνὸς πολλὰ δοξάσαι ἀδύνατον, Parm. 166, B., 9th Prop.

Note *, p. 57.—As to the Platonic scheme as a residual expedient, *vide* Soph. 252, E.-253, A. As to the dependence of things on The One, *vide* Arist. Metaph. A. (I.) 6: τὸ ἓν = οὐσία, τὸ μέγα καὶ τὸ μικρὸν = ὕλη. See, also, sect. Participation, and notes.

Note *, p. 59.—As to rest being the absolute element, *vide* Soph. 249, B.–C.; *cf.* Phædr. 247, A.; Crat. 401, A.-D. It has no communion with motion, Soph. 254, D. In Rep. vii. the preparatory studies are ranged as follows: arithmetic, geometry, the science of surfaces, and the science of solids; then astronomy, the science of the motion of solids. The latter is chiefly valuable, as it tends to fix our thoughts on real rest and motion. But, as time does not bind reality (sect. Participation,) it is conceived that real rest and motion denote the elements of the higher existences, ὁ θεὸς καὶ αὐτὸ τὸ τῆς ζωῆς εἶδος, Phæd. 106, D. If this be so, we can see why Plato attributed circular motion to Νοῦς, Tim. 34, A.; for mathematics are not pure knowledge, Rep. vii. 533, C. D., but they come nearest it, *ib.* Hence, perpetual energy, or power of self-modification, Leg. x. 896, A, would be in mathematical terms circular; *cf.* κίνησις δ' οὐκ ἔστι συνεχής, ἀλλ' ἡ κατὰ τόπον καὶ ταύτης ἡ εὐκλῳ, Arist. Metaph. Λ. (XII.) 6.; *cf.* Tim. 34, A. Mr. Grote considers that the Sophistes breaks down the barrier between *Fientia* and *Entia*, viz., motion; ib. 459; but it is conceived that sensible motion, in Plato's opinion, meant that the sequent A disappeared or vanished into sequent B; while noetic motion, as in the case of the Eidetic Numbers, meant progression according to the order of thought; each moment in the process being distinct, and never merging its individuality in the next: *vide* Essay, pp. 67-68, and notes.

Note *, p. 61.—Soph. 254, D.; the text down to n. * is founded on Soph. 254, B.-259, E., inclusive.

Note *, p. 64.—Soph. 248, E. 249, C.; Phil. 30, C. D. From these passages and the Platonic law of cognition the inference in the text has been derived.

Note *, p. 65.—There is an efficient cause of combination, Phileb. 23, D. This is The Good, the cause of all good things, Rep. vii. 517,

B.–C.; cf. Epin. 981, B; Crat. 416, C.–D.; Rep. ii. 380, C.; Theæt. 176, A.; and it is ἀληθινὸν καὶ θεῖον Νοῦν, Phil. 22, C. As to the 10, vide Arist. Phys. iii. 6, 6.; Metaph. Λ. (XII.) 8. The rationale of the Ten given in the text, is not at variance with Aristotle's statement that it consists of two Pentads, Metaph. M. 7. For the elements of the Idea are per se two monads. But the relation between the two monads is diversity, which is also a monad, Parm. 143, B. That is, the elements out of relation = 2 monads; in relation = 3 monads; and out of and in relation, each state being considered as distinct = 5 monads. But as the Indefinite is per se incogitable, it must be given in some determinate relation and when given in relation, its actual relativity, and previous non-relativity, or indefiniteness are apparent, Parm. 158, E.–159 A. Now to express the joint state, a third set of monads come in. Hence elements out of all relation are two monads, and elements in relation are three monads, the two states considered as several, are five monads, and the two states considered in combination are five monads in addition. That is, 5 + 5 = 10. It is evident that 10 is the maximum; for the elements must be either in relation, or out of relation, or both. But the Idea as a result presupposes the numbers given in the text, and in apprehending them, the 10 or binary pentad energies. As to the rationale of numbers, vid. Parm. 143-144 A.; Arist. Met. M. 7. It should be remarked that the numbers are objective states, while the monads are the moments they contain. In the same way the psychic principle is 10, the psychological numbers are 10, and the mathematical are also 10. But, as 1 is the number of pure unmodified knowledge, νοῦς, Arist. de Anim. I. 2, 9, the psychic principle in its ultimate relation to the Deity constitutes 10. Since, knowledge being the indifference of subject and object, subject = 10 = object = 10 = indifference = 10. As to the noetic numbers being ἀσύμβλητοι inter se, see Arist. Metaph. M. (XIII.) 6; αἱ δ' (μονάδες) ἐν τῇ Δυάδι αὐτῇ πρὸς τὰς ἐν τῇ Τριάδι αὐτῇ ἀσύμβλητοι.

Note⁹, p. 71.—Each element preserves its individuality, Parm. 158, E.–159, A.; ib. 159, D.; the metaphor is taken from

Soph. 246, A. B., and the passage shows that solidity was deemed to be the objective quality, and that the opposite school argued, κατὰ σμικρὰ διαθραύοντες ἐν τοῖς λόγοις, i. e. substituted analysis for Common Sense.

Note ⁱ⁰, p. 73.—The Sun is the physical analogue of The Good, Rep. vi. 509, B. Hence, perhaps, taking in consideration Plato's connexion with Philolaus, the mythical statement in the Timæus, that the virtuous soul will return εἰς τὴν τοῦ ξυννόμου οἴκησιν ἄστρου, 42, B. The Good being the sun, its consequents are stars, κατὰ τοὺς εἰκότας λόγους.

Against Plato's Idea *Boni*, Mr. Grote urges three objections:— The first is, that he does not in the Republic tell us what it is, iii. 241. But Plato tells us that The Good cannot be seen at present; that it is a matter of inference, συλλογίστεα, κ. τ. λ., Rep. xii. 517, C.; and in the same book, Socrates, though abounding in good will, declares that Glauco will be unable to follow him in the dialectic ascent, οὐδ᾽ εἰκόνα ἂν ἔτι οἷ λέγομεν ἴδοις, ἀλλ᾽ αὐτὸ τ᾽ ἀληθές; that is, The Good is an object of intuition, and cannot be depicted in sensuous colours, εἰκόνες. Each man must see for himself, which he cannot do fully here, but will hereafter, *vide* n. ˡ. The second objection is, that "the word [*Bonum*] has no meaning except in relation to some apprehending subject," *ib.* p. 242, n. *a*. This is quite true; but does it show that *Bonum* must be altered and modified by plenary cognition—by its being known as it is; that is, by our knowing all that is to be known, and leaving nothing unknown? The third objection is, that Plato's identification of *Unum* and *Bonum* is "a forced conjunction of two disparaties"—of a metaphysical and of an ethical element, *ib.* 475, n. *a*. Now, it is conceived, it is one of Plato's pre-eminent merits as a thinker, that he does not regard a human being as a mere reasoning machine, but as a compound of reason and emotion. If, then, man be a compound being, The Good must satisfy his compound nature, and not leave one half ungratified. The Good must be, in Butler's language, a subject of the understanding, and an object of the heart. In fact, Plato's meaning appears to be, that personality is indivisible, but not simple. With regard to the Platonic End, Mr. Grote observes, that "in an ethical discourse about *Summum Bonum*, the antithesis between Pleasure and Intelligence, on which the Philebus turns, is from the outset illogical. What gives it its apparent plausibility is, that the exercise of Intelligence has pleasures and pains of its own, and includes therefore in itself a part of the End, besides being the constant and indispensable directing force or means," ii. 595. Now, the question raised in the Philebus is between Pleasure in the technical Platonic sense and Prudence, or the ethical and cognitive faculty, Phil. 11., B.–C., to which Plato allocates pleasures of its own, Rep. ix. 585, D.–E.; but which pleasures are different in kind from the satisfactions of the senses. Hence Prudence, *qud* containing end, and means, Phæd. 69, A. B., is contrasted with the objects of the appetites, which are properly only alleviations of pain, Phil. 31, D. Rep. iv. 437, E.–438, B. Pleasure is of the Indefinite, Phil. 31, D.—of the More and Less, and cannot be attributed to higher existences, Phil. 33, B. See the section on Justice.

SECTION VI.

Note ¹, p. 74.—Tim. 61, E.

Note ², p. 75.— *Vide* n. ¹, Sect. II.; as to pleasure, *vide* Phileb. 31, A.

Note ³, p. 76.—Phæd. 64, A. C.; 65, A.; 67, A.

Note ⁴, p. 80.—The view of Time and Space given in the text is derived as follows:—Aristotle states that Plato's theory of time is unique: ἀλλὰ μὴν περί γε χρόνου ἔξω ἑνὸς ὁμονοητικῶς ἔχοντες φαίνονται πάντες ἀγέννητον γὰρ εἶναι λέγουσι. Πλάτων τὰ αὐτὸν γεννᾷ μόνος, Phys. viii. 1, 10. Aristotle then refers to the Timæus, Χρόνος δ᾽ οὖν μετ᾽ οὐρανοῦ γέγονεν, 38, B. Now, the continuation of the passage is, ἵνα ἅμα γεννηθέντες ἅμα καὶ λ δ θ ω σ ι ν, and γέννα is the technical term for the result of the combination of the πέρας and the ἄπειρον, Phil. 25, D.; the meaning of γένεσις will be discussed in the next section.

The peculiarity of Plato's theory appears to have been the

mixture of the Heracleitan and Pythagorean views. Aristotle says that the Pythagoreans held the Triad to be objective, παρὰ τῆς φύσεως εἰληφότες ὥσπερ νόμους ἐκείνης, de Cœl. A. i. 1; Br. 268, a, 10-13; and that the Triad denoted Beginning, Middle, and End. Now, to Heracleitus, objectivity has no meaning; everything was γένεσις. But Plato allows the objectivity of the Now, Tim. 37, E.-38, A, and contrasts it with the past and future, *ib.*, and this view is worked out in the third proposition of the Parmenides, 155, E.-157, D. Plato himself seems to wish to indicate his originality by twice using the word ἄτοπον, *ib.* 156, D. The same theory in a more concrete form is found in Phæd. 71; *cf.* Leg. x. 893, E.-894, A. In fact, the view of Time indicated is merely a case of Plato's ἓν καὶ πολλά; as to space, vide Tim. 62, A. D., τρίτον δέ, κ. τ. λ.; and for the definition of ὀνείρωξις therein, *vide* Rep. v. 476, C.; and *cf.* text, pp. 87-90.

Note ⁵, p. 80.—Tim. 52, B. D. As to the priority of the Noetic, *vide* Epin. 980, D. E.; *cf.* Leg. x. 892, A.; Tim. 34, B.-C.

Note ⁶, (*ib*).—Τούτῳ μὲν οὖν τῷ γένει, (sc. τῇ στιγμῇ) καὶ διεμάχετο Πλάτων ὡς ὄντι γεωμετρικῷ δόγματι· ἀλλ' ἐκάλει ἀρχὴν γραμμῆς. Τοῦτο δὲ πολλάκις ἐτίθει τὰς ἀτόμους γραμμάς, Metaph. A, (i). 7.

Note ⁷, p. 81.—Arist. de Anima, i. 2, 9; Metaph. N. 3.

Note ⁸, p. 82.—Arist. Metaph. A. (ι.) 6.

Note ⁹, p. 83.—In the beginning of the Parmenides, all empirical modes of conceiving Participation, viz.: Inherence, whether total or partial, 131, A. E.; *cf.* Phil. 15, B.; Soph. 253, D. E.; Similarity in any mode, whether subjective, 132, A, or objective, 132, D.; *cf.* Rep. x. 597, C.; Tim. 31, A., are rejected; at the same time, the total separation of the two elements is refuted, while Ideas are pointed out as the proper object of dialectic, Parm. 135, B. C.; *cf.* Phil. 15, C. It follows then, it is conceived, that The Idea is not subject to modes of empirical apprehension, and that it is not totally isolated; *cf.* Arist. Phys. iv. 2, 5.

SECTION VII.

Note ¹, p. 84.—Arist. Phys. iv. 2, 2.
Note ², p. 85.—Μέθεξις = μίμησις, Arist. Metaph. A, (I.) 6.
Note ³, p. 87.—ψεῦδον, ἐνι τε καὶ ἀλήθη, Rep. ii. 377, A.
Note ⁴, p. 88.—Rep. v. 476, C. D.; cf. Tim. 52, B. C.
Note ⁵, p. 91.—Arist. Phys. iii. 4, 2; Metaph. M. 6., N. 3.
Note ⁶, p. 93.—ὁμοίως γὰρ φασι τόδε τὰ διαγράμματα γράφουσι, Arist. de Cœl, 279, b, 32; and Simplic. 488, b. 15.
Note ⁷, p. 94.—Tim. pp. 54-55, C.
Note ⁸, p. 97.—The circle is apparently derived from the fragment of Parmenides, ap. Soph. 244, E. These verses also contain, perhaps, the germ of the More and Less, οὔτε τι μεῖζον οὔτε τι βαιότερον. The physical elements Fire and Earth are due to Parmenides, Arist. Phys. I. 5, 1; and the Three is the Pythagorean Number of Fire, Metaph. N. 5. Three was also the number of the Definite τὸ πᾶν καὶ τὰ πάντα τοῖν Τρισὶ ὥρισται, Arist. de Cœl. i. 1. Hence the triangle is the superficial symbol of the definitive and formative agent. Two was the Number of Earth and of the Indefinite, ib. 3 Met. N, 5; and the square their superficial symbol. Hence, the necessity, according to Pythagorean notions, of trisecting the right angle. As to the geometrical character of arithmetic, vide Theæt. 147, E.-148, A. B., and vide n. ¹³, p. 128.

Note ⁹, p. 98.—Tim. 54, E.-55, A.
Note ¹⁰, p. 99—Ib. 55, A.; Arist. Phys. I. 6, 5. With regard to the Icosihedron, ib. 55, B.; as to the Dodecahedron, assuming it to be constructed in the same way, it would be 6 x 6 x 2. As to the propriety of identifying it with æther, Plato says πότερον ἐὰ ἵνα ἢ πέντε αὐτοὺς ἀληθείᾳ. ... μᾶλλον ἂν ταύτῃ στὰς εἰκότως διαπορήσαι, Tim. 55, D.; cf. Epin. 984, B. C. Xenocrates mentions πέντε σχήματα καὶ σώματα. The Dodecahedron may have suggested the δωδεκάσκυτοι σφαῖραι of Phæd. 110, B. Æther is also contrasted with air, ib. 109, B. C.

As to the non-locality of The Idea, vid. Arist. Phys. iv. 2, 5,

Πλάτων μόνος Διαιρέων—διά τι οὐκ ἐν τούτῳ τὰ εἴδη καὶ οἱ ἀριθμοί κ. τ. λ. cf. Phys. iii. 42.

Note ¹¹, p. 103.—Arist. de Cœl. i. 1. As to the Demiurgic function of Νοῦς, vide Epin. ὃ μέσῳ πλάττων καὶ δημιουργῶν προσίκει, 981, B., and Tim. 68, D. As to the contest of the Demiurge with Necessity, cf. Epist. vii. 343, A.; Parm. 158, E.; also the Myth in the Protagoras. Epimetheus, the finisher of animals, which were formed of fire and earth, was οὐ πάνυ τι σοφός; and his gifts are all accompanied by analogous deficiencies, Protag. 320, C.- 321, C.

Note ¹², p. 106.—Polit. 269, D.-275, D.; Phileb. 18, A. B. If the sensible indefinite be conceived as a right line, and the monad as a point, then the inverted regime of Cronus, will ἐπὶ σμικροτάτων βαίνων ποδὸς ἶναι, Polit. 270, Δ. This particular, pointed out by Mr. Grote, II. p. 481, n. *s.*, was overlooked in the composition of the text, but confirms, it is conceived, the explanation attempted there.

Note ¹³, p. 108.—Parm. 132, D.-133, A.

Note ¹⁴.—Arist. Meteorol. ii. 2. As to The Good, vide Eth. N. i., 6; Eth. Eud. L 8. Aristotle's criticisms of the Idea *Boni* are all directed from the empirical standing-point, whereas Plato's Good is the most transcendental of entities, Rep. vi. 509, B.

Note ¹⁵.—Arist. Eth. N. iii. 4, 4; cf. Metaph. K, 6; as to the canon of objectivity, vide Eth. N. x. 2, 4. The *Primum Movens* is devoid of extension, Phys. viii. 10, 9.

SECTION VIII.

Note ¹, p. 113.—As the sanctions of the θυμός attach to the transgressions of the ἐπιθυμία, Rep. iv. 439, E.-440, A, it would seem that the θυμός is mortal; cf. Tim. 69, C.-72, D. The charioteer, Phædr. 253, D. E., represents Prudence, the unruly horse Appetence, and the good horse their Indifference, which partakes of both extremes; and the words εἰκῇ συμπεφυρμένος, applied to the dark horse, allude to the ἄπειρος = φορά. The θυμός, as it regards appetence, is phenomenal and mortal; but as it partakes of φρόνησις is noetic and immortal. As to the sentimental element, with Phædr. 254, E. cf. 238, B. C., εἰ γὰρ ἄνευ λόγου—ἔρως ἀληθής.

Note ¹, p. 114.—The tripartite division in Rep. iv. 436, is psychological, εἰ τῷ αὐτῷ τούτῳ ἕκαστα πράττομεν ἢ τρισὶν οὖσιν ἄλλο ἄλλῳ, A. Cf. ib. ἢ ἰλη τῇ ψυχῇ; as to the meaning of σῶμα and χρήματα, vide Phæd. 66, B. D.; cf. Rep. ix. 580, D. E. Phæd. 69, A.-B., explains the relation of vulgar utilitarianism to Plato' Ethics. No men except philosophers have φρόνησις in esse. The virtue of other men consists in measuring phenomenal pleasures and pains with others of the same kind. They forego one pleasure through desire of another, 69, A.; and so of courage, cf. Protag. 360, B. They deal in money, Phæd. 69, A.; that is, with the representative media of exchange, and not with φρόνησις, the paramount ethical item and standard of ethical value; cf. Lach. 192, E.; while the scientific utilitarian knows the comparative worth of all the items, Rep. ix. 582, A. B.; Lach. 199, D. This state is the result of science, Gorg. 500, A.; cf. δίκαιος καὶ ὅσιος μετὰ φρονήσεως γίνεται, Theæt. 176, A. B.

Note ², p. 114.—Phileb. 35, E.; Phædr. 258, E.

Note, ³, p. 115.—Phileb. 51, B. E.-52, C.; as to their object, vide Lys. 221, D. E.; Phileb. 34, E.-35, A., sq.; Rep. iv. 439, A.

Note ⁴, p. 116; Protag. 355, D. E.-356, A. B. 357, B. 353, D.-E. 354, A. D.

Note ⁵, p. 117.—Gorg. 500, A.; Rep. ix. 582, A. B.

Note ⁶, p. 118.—Phileb. 13, A. B.; 32, D. As to pure pleasure, ib. 51, B. Mr. Grote, II, p. 607, n. x., excepts to Plato's view that the pleasures of mathematics are not preceded by want, Ph. 52, A. But Plato is talking of natural, and not acquired feelings: ἡμεῖς αὐτὰ τὰ τῆς φύσεως μόνον παθήματα χωρὶς τοῦ λογισμοῦ διαπραίνωμεν, ib. 52, B. The formula of appetite is a desire of the means of relief for the sake of relief, because of the presence of the special evil, Lys. 218, E.; that is, without the pain of hunger there can be no pleasure in food; but there is no precedent want which impels a child to learn, as a precedent want impels it to look for food. Plato also divides pleasures and pains into true and false, with reference to their effects relatively—to (1) the Deity, Phil. 39, E.; to (2) our hopes and fears, *ib.* 41, E.–42, A.; (3) to each other, *i. e.*, the law of sequence, *ib.* 38, C. D.—*i. e.*, to (1) the purely objective; to (2) the purely subjective; and to (3) their compromise. As to the hierarchy, see Text, pp. 149–51, and note.

Note *, p. 120.—As to the relation of κάλλος, ἀρετὴ, and ὀρθότης to χρεία, *vid.* Rep. x. 601, D.; *cf.* Gorg. 474, D. E.; 506, D.; Rep. i. 352, E.; 353, A. E., and the illustrations in the Hippias Maj. Even immortality has its special utility, Euthyd. 289, B.; and likewise the Regal Art, *ib.* 292, A. The highest category is that which we like *propter se* and *propter aliud*, Rep. ii. 358, A. That there must be some ultimate end, *vid.* Lys. 218, D.; 219, C. D.; 220, A.; Lach. 185, D.; Gorg. 499, E.; 500, A.; Symp. 210, E.; Phil. 65, A.

Note *, p. 122.—The Gorgias, it is conceived, developes Plato's view of the relation of the empirical objects of Ethics to the spiritual efficient, or agent. Beneficial pleasures are good, *ib.* 503, C. D. The question, then, is—is it better to do a wrong, or suffer it? Socrates answers. Βουλοίμην μὲν ἂν ἔγωγε οὐδέτερα, εἰ δ' ἀναγκαῖον ἢν ἀδικεῖν ἢ ἀδικεῖσθαι, ἑλοίμην ἂν μᾶλλον ἀδικεῖσθαι ἢ ἀδικεῖν, Gorg. 469, B. C.; and the reason is, μὴ ἐγχρονισθῇ τὸ νόσημα τῆς ἀδικίας ὕπουλον τὴν ψυχὴν ποιήσῃ καὶ ἀνίατον, 480, B. Now, ἀνίατος is the Platonic metaphor for eternal misery, *ib.* 525, C.; Phæd. 113, E.; Rep. x. 615, E. Mr. Grote objects, that the Platonic metaphor overlooks an all-important difference between bodily illness and spiritual disease:—"The taint or distemper with which Archelaus is supposed to inoculate himself, when he commits signal crime, is a pure fancy or poetical metaphor on the part of Plato himself. A distemper must imply something painful, enfeebling, disabling to the individual who feels it; there is no other meaning; we cannot recognise a distemper which does not make itself felt in any way by the distempered person," II., p. 111. That Archelaus was not aware of his spiritual κακία, *i. e.*, ἀδικία, Plato holds, 471, D; but this is the worst feature in the case; it is of the very essence of his punishment, Theæt. 176, E.-177, A.; Leg. v. 728, B; and *cf.* the doctrine, οὐδεὶς ἑκὼν κακός. Plato would compare the state of Archelaus, not to actual chronic uneasiness, but to idiocy, or lunacy, in which the patient was quite happy.

Note. ¹⁰, p. 122.—Rep. vi., 505, A.; vii. 509, C.; Phil. 65, A. As to other objects of the Eros, see Symp. 210, 211. As to its subjective side, φρόνησις, *vid. ib.* 206, A.; 209, A.; *cf.* Phædr. 241, A. D.; Lys. 222, A.; Leg. viii. 837, A. D.

Note ¹¹, p. 127.—Ethical training is a καθαρμός, Soph. 227, D.; 230, D. As to Justice, *vid.* Rep. 433, B. C. As to Prudence, Temperance, and Fortitude, *vid.* Rep. iv. 442, C. D.; Lach. 199, D. E.; Leg. 631, C.; 632, C., 963, A. The empirical objects of ethics are mere occasions for evoking φρόνησις, Phæd. 69, A. D.; the correlate of κάλλος, Symp. 203, C. D.; and of God, Theæt. 176, A. C. Mr. Grote (iii. 164–5) objects, that the theory of Justice in the Republic overlooks the difficulties started in other Dialogues; but they, it is conceived, deal with other matters. Thus the Theætetus discusses what is ἐπιστήμη, and not what is φρόνησις, the moral faculty or organ, 146, E.; while the Laches and Charmides discuss explanations different from those given in the Republic, although the verbal definition be the same; Lach. 190, E., *et sqq.*; Charm. 161, E., *et sqq.*

Note ¹², 128.—Rep. ii. 369, A.; 372, E.; Rep. iv. 420, D. C.; 430, C.; 431, A. D.; 432, A.; 433, D.; 434, D. E.; 435, E.; 441, A. C.; 442, D. E.; 443, B. C.; 445, A. C.; Rep. v. 449, A. D.; 462, D. C.; 472, B. D.; Rep. vi. 484, D.; Rep. vii. 541, D.; Rep. viii. 543, D.; 545, A. D. C.; 548, D.; 550, C. D.; 553, E.; 554, D.; 555, A. B.; 558, C.; 559, D. E.; 561, E.; 564, A.; 565, D.; Rep. ix. 571, A.; 574, E.; 576, C.; 577, C.; 578, A.; 579, C.; 580, C. D.; 588, D.; 592, A.; Rep. x. 605, D.; 612, C. The Republic represents the ideal of the virtuous man, not realized on earth, ἐν οὐρανῷ ἴσως παράδειγμα ἀνάκειται τῷ βουλομένῳ ὁρᾶν καὶ ὁρῶντι ἑαυτὸν κατοικίζειν, Rep. ix. 592, B.; the Leges, then, would represent the best human or actual polity, the Timocracy of the Republic (viii.); for, τοῦ ἀρίστου δόξαν, ὥσπερ ἂν ἴσεσθαι τούτων ἡγήσωνται πόλις εἴτε ἰδιῶταί τινες, ἐὰν αὐτὴ ἡματοῦσα ἐν ψυχαῖς διακοσμῇ πάντα ἄνδρα, κἂν σφάλληταί τι, δίκαιον μὲν εἶναι φατέον τὸ ταύτῃ πραχθέν, κ. τ. λ., Leg. ix. 864, A. As to the numbers, *vid*. Theæt. 148, B., κατὰ τὸν τοῦ μήκους ἀριθμὸν, Rep. ix. 587, D. The tyrant's pleasure is a plane number, 3 × 3 = 9, and 9, κατὰ δὲ δυνάμιν καὶ τρίτην αὔξην, = 9^3 = 729. The same mode of conception may account for Plato's habit of multiplying words to intensify his meaning; such as ὅ ἐστιν, ὄντως ὄν.

Note [13], p. 132.—Euthyp. 5, D.; 6, D.; Arist. Met. A. (I.) 7; *ib*. M. 4; in both passages he urges that there should be also Ideas τῶν φθαρτῶν, κατὰ δὲ τὸ νοεῖν τι φθαρέντος. But Plato would not admit that we νοοῦμεν τὰ φθαρτά, but δοξάζομεν.

Note [14], p. 134.—As to the myths, *vid*. Phædr. 248, A. B.; Gorg. 524, D.; 525, A.; *vid*. Leg. x. 904, B. C.

Note [15], p. 135.—Theæt. 176, A.; Rep. ii. 379, B.–380, B. C. There is no retributive punishment; *vide* Protag. 324, A. B.; Gorg. 525, B.; Leg. 933, E.–934, B.; 728, B. C. The Divine Will is not altered by prayer or sacrifice, Alc. ii. 149, E.–150, A.; Leg. iv. 716, D.; Leg. x. 906, A.–907, B. As to the regulation of worship, *vide* Leg. x. 909, D., *sq*.

Note [16], p. 139.—Ἀνάγκη, Tim. 48, A. No sensible sequent is καθ' αὑτό, but is in consequence of being an ἐφίμενον ἄλλου, Phil. 53, D.

Note [17], p. 140.—Phædr. 245, C. D. As to the seeming exception to οὐδεὶς ἑκὼν ἄδικος, *vide* Protag. 352, B.–358, C. D.

Note [18], p. 142.—As to the sensible method, *vide* Parm. 135, E.–136, A.; and as to its contrast with the noetic, Rep. vi. 511, B.; *cf*. Aristotle's remark, Eth. Nich. i. 4, 5, which appears to allude to the noetic process, εἴδεσιν αὐτοῖς δι' αὐτῶν εἰς αὐτά, καὶ εἰς εἴδη, Rep. vi., 511, C., as Plato would not have termed anything sensible ἀρχή.

Note [20], p. 144.—Phileb. 16, D. E.

Note [21], p. 145.—As to the letters, *vide* Phileb. 18, B. D.; as to knowledge of contraries, *vide* Hipp. Min.; *pass*. Ion, 532, A.; Rep. i. 333, E.–334, A.; Symp. 223, D. As to Parts and Ideas, *vide* Polit. 263, B., and Xenocrates, ap. Simplic. τὰ μὲν οὖν ζῷα οὕτω πάλιν διῃρεῖτο ις ἰδέας καὶ μέρη . . . . . ἕως εἰς τὰ πάντων στοιχεῖα ἀφίκετο τῶν ζώων ἃ δὴ πέντε σχήματα καὶ σώματα ὠνόμαζεν, Br. 427, a 17, sq.

Note ⁿ, p. 147.—As Sight is the paramount sense, Rep. 507, E. 508; and as the noetic faculty acts intuitively, Plato naturally gives the object of that faculty a name borrowed from the sense. 'Ιδέα properly denotes appearance, considered as a result of details, Phæd. 108, D.-109, B.; Amatores, 132, A.; Protag. 315, E.; Alc. i. 119, C.; Charm. 157. D.; 158, A.; 175, D.; Politic. 291, B.; Rep. ii. 380, D. (ter); 588, C. (bis); D.; Phædr. 251, A. But, as the result is, in Aristotelian language, the final cause of the disposition of the elements, 'Ιδέα passed from its proper sense into that of structural type; and the notion structural type, viewed from the subjective side, would be construed as the ultimate efficient; and, viewed from the objective side, as the ultimate manifestation of objectivity. Hence, the order of the various shades of meaning may be given as follows:—
(1) appearance as a result, as in the passages cited above;
(2) appearance as a type, Phileb. 67, A.; Hipp. Maj. 297, B.;*
(3) appearance conceived as a typical efficient, and consequently

---

* The words ἐν πατρὸς ἰδίᾳ taken in connexion with Tim. 50, D., προσεικάσαι πρέπει τὸ δ' ὅθεν πατρί, suggest an explanation of the lines,

ἐς τόδε σεσήμενει στέγος
Φάος τόδ' οὐκ ἄπαππον Ἰδαίου πυρὸς . . .
Νικᾷ δ' ὁ πρῶτος καὶ τελευταῖος δραμών.

Ag. 309, sqq.

Æschylus combines two ways of stating the fact, that the watchman saw the signal. The common sense view is, that the watch saw the fire which was lit last; but Æschylus, as a Pythagorean, refers the entire series to the beacon on Ida, as the efficient, οὐκ ἄπαππον. The successive kindling of the beacons suggests the torch race, as each when lit seems to leave the others behind; and he finally combines the two views in the language of the race, "the fire on Ida is the victor (acc. Pythagoras), although, καὶ (in matter of fact), the last in the race," because first kindled. The same view of causation may be traced in the term εἶδος applied to the relation of dust and mud, ib. 491, and to that of fire and smoke; Theb. 479; cf. Plat. Tim. 50, D., τὴν δὲ μεταξὺ τούτων φύσιν λεγόνων.

as to the percipient the final reality, Euthyp. 5, D.; 6, C. D.; Phæd. 104, B. D. (*bis*), E. 105, D.; Theæt. 184, D.; 203, C. E.; 204, A.; 205, C. D.; Soph. 235, D.; 253, D.; 254, A.; 255, E.; Crat. 389, E.; 418, E. 439, E.; Phileb. 16, D. (*bis*), 21, B.; 60, D.; 64, A. E.; Polit. 258, C.; 262, B.; 289, B.; 307, C.; 308, C.; Rep. 369, A.; 479, A.; 466, D.; 505, A.; 507, B. (*bis*), E.; 508, E.; 517, B.; 526, E.; 534, D.; 544, D.; 596, B. (*ter*); Leg. viii. 836, D.; xii. 965, C.; Tim. 28, A.; 35, A.; 39, E.; 40, A.; 46, C.; 49, C.; 50, E.; 57, B.; 58, D.; 59, C.; 60, B.; 70, C.; 71, A.; 77, A.; Parm. 132, A. C.; 133, C.; 134, C.; 135, A. D.; 157, D.; Symp. 196, A.; 204, C.; Phædr. 237, D.-238, A.; 246, A.; 265, D.; 273, E. The shades of meaning, in the third class of passages cited, are blended in different degrees; but, it is conceived, the notion type, when understood with the above qualifications, will suit them all. On the other hand, as to Plato, noetic appearance and noetic reality were identical, the word is singularly appropriate. As to the identity of the Idea and the Beautiful, *vide* note ', p. 120.

Note ", p. 147.—Rep. x. 597, C.; *cf.* Parm. 132, A. B. E. 133 A.; Tim. 31, A.

Note ", p. 148.—Arist. de Anima, I. 2, 9.

Note ", (*ib.*).—Rep. x. 598, A. B.; 602, D.; 603, B.; Polit. 284, E.; Euthyp. 7, C.; Epin. 977, C. D.

Note ", p. 151.—Phil. 66.*

Note " (*ib.*).—Theæt. 176, A.

*Ἡδονή κτῆμα οὐκ ἔστι πρῶτον οὐδ᾽ αὖ δεύτερον, ἀλλὰ πρῶτον μὲν τῇ περὶ μέτρον καὶ τὸ μέτριον καὶ καίριον καὶ πάντα ὁπόσα τοιαῦτα χρὴ νομίζειν τὴν ἀΐδιον ᾑρῆσθαι φύσιν. Π. Φαίνεται γοῦν ἐκ τῶν νῦν λεγομένων. Σ. Δεύτερον μὴν περὶ τὸ σύμμετρον καὶ καλὸν καὶ τὸ τέλεον καὶ ἱκανὸν καὶ πάνθ᾽ ὁπόσα τῆς γενεᾶς αὖ ταύτης ἐστίν. Π. Ἔοικε γοῦν. Σ. Τὸ τοίνυν τρίτον, ὡς ἡ ἐμὴ μαντεία, νοῦν καὶ φρόνησιν τιθεὶς οὐκ ἂν μέγα τι τῆς ἀληθείας παρεξέλθοις. Π. Ἴσως. Σ. Ἆρ᾽ οὖν οὐ τέταρτα, ἃ τῆς ψυχῆς αὐτῆς ἔθεμεν, ἐπιστήμας τε καὶ τέχνας καὶ δόξας ὀρθὰς λεχθείσας, ταῦτ᾽ εἶναι τὰ πρὸς τοῖς τρισὶ τέταρτα, εἴπερ τοῦ ἀγαθοῦ ἐστι μᾶλλον τῆς ἡδονῆς ἐγγενῆ. Π. Τάχ᾽ ἄν. Σ. Πέμπτας τοίνυν, ἃς ἡδονὰς ἔθεμεν ἀλύπους ὁρισάμενοι, καθαρὰς ἐπονομάσαντες τῆς ψυχῆς αὐτῆς, ἐπιστήμαις, ταῖς δὲ αἰσθήσεσιν, ἑπομένας.

SECTION IX.

Note ¹, p. 152.—Phæd. 96, B.; 115, C.; Rep. v. 469, D.; Gorg. 525, B.

Note ², p. 153.—Men. 81, B. D.; Phæd. 72, E.–73, A.; Phædr. 250, C. According to Mr. Grote, "As the doctrine is stated in the Menon, it is made applicable to all minds, instead of being confined, as in Phædrus, Phædo, and elsewhere, to a few highly gifted minds," ii. p. 19. But Plato holds, it is conceived, that immortality *in posse* belongs to every human soul, Phædr. 251, B.; 249, B.–E.; and, in the Phædo, the state of the soul after death hinges upon the relation between the higher and lower elements here; and upon the preponderance of the former plenary immortality is made dependent, 81, A–82, B. C.; but with regard to inferior immortality, how far the myths and the doctrine of metempsychosis denote a lower state

The opinions of Ast, Schleiermacher, Trendelenburg, and Stallbaum, may be found in Dr. Badham's Philebus, together with his own view of the passage, Præf. pp. xlv.–xlviii. In opposition to these high authorities, the writer rests his interpretation, first, on the simplicity of the antithesis between the objective and the subjective; and second, on the text itself. The word κτῆμα denotes *a thing to be held by some one*; and the two first grades of κτήματα are said to be περί, while the three last are said to be identical with, certain things specified; that is, the act of acquisition in grades 1 and 2 is distinct from the thing acquired; but in 3, 4, and 5, is identical with it, or rather is another phase of the acquirer. But this is precisely the distinction between an objective-object and a subjective-object. The words χρὴ νομίζειν, as is evident from the reply of Protarchus, refer to the previous discussion of the nature and affinities of Φρονήσις and Ἡδονή, Phil. 65–66; so that the passage is really equivalent to ὁπόσα τοιαῦτα τὴν ἀΐδιον βρηνται φύσιν, and may therefore be rendered, "all such things as have taken on themselves the eternal Nature," *i. e.*, are such, because they have taken on themselves, the eternal Nature. This rendering agrees with Trendelenburg's translation, "quidquid ejusmodi æternam naturam suscepisse credendum est," save that τοιαῦτα is taken proleptically and the interpretation is different. Dr. Badham's objections apply to both renderings, and are as follows :—" In the first place, ὁπόσα χρὴ τοιαῦτα νομίζειν κ. λ. cannot be taken thus; for this would be expressed by ὁπόσα, τοιοῦτ' ὄντα, χρὴ νομίζειν— and though the order might be changed, the participle would be indispensable. But, even if we conceded such an interpretation, what would become of πρῶτον of existence in time, cannot be made out with certainty. Plato evidently was perplexed by the case of infants, Rep. x. 615, C.

Note⁵, p. 153.—Phædr. 245, C. E.

Note⁶, p. 154.—The αὐτά do not admit γένεσις of ἀλλήλων, Phæd. 103, B.; ib., 105, A. The higher existences Θεός, καὶ αὐτὸ τὸ τῆς ζωῆς εἶδος καὶ εἴ τι ἄλλο ἀθάνατόν ἐστι, are imperishable, i. e. do not yield to decay. ib. 106, D.

Note⁶, p. 154.—Rep. x. 608, D.-610, E.

Note⁶, p. 155.—Phæd. 93, A.; 94, C.; Rep. 610, C.

Note⁷ (ib.).—Phæd. 80, A.; 94, C. D.

Note⁸ (ib.).—Phæd. 71, E.

Note⁹, p. 156.—As to the relation of the phenomenal to the non-phenomenal, vid. Text, pp. 74-83, and notes.

Note¹⁰, p. 157.—As to individuality, vide Alc. i. 130, A. D.; 131, A.; Phæd. 115, C.; vide Mansel's Proleg. Log., 2nd ed. pp. 139-40; Mill's Hamilton, pp. 212-3; and Whately's Logic, Remarks on voc. "Same," Part III.

μὲν τῇ περὶ μέτρον? It is obvious that, in such a case, περὶ has no meaning nor construction. But, above all, such an expression as, "to have adopted (or received) the eternal nature," is at variance with the whole method of Plato. For if the Good is to be sought for in them, it must be because they are emanations or productions of it; whereas, according to this view, the Good is superadded to them, and that through their seeking it. But no one conversant with the language will understand ᾑρῆσθαι in the sense of παρειληφέναι, or still less of εἰληχέναι. And then, again, why have we the perfect? In speaking of a fact which has no reference to any particular time, the only proper tense would have been ἑλέσθαι. Those who feel these objections will not need to have them confirmed by a consideration of the unsuitableness of the sense thus extorted from them; and yet the sense is in itself very objectionable, because it would amount to this—that Plato, having sought by a laborious argument for that which had most affinity with the Good, at last found it—in the Idea of the Good." Now, ὄντα would spoil the sense, as it would imply that, already being so and so, they had taken on the eternal Nature; whereas the meaning contended for is, that they are so and so, because they have taken; as in the same dialogue, we have προσαγορεύεις αὐτ᾽ ἀνόμοί ὄνθ᾽ ἑτέρῳ ὀνόματι, Phil. 19, A.; that is, you call things which are already dissimilar by a different name. With regard to πρῶτον μὲν τῇ περὶ μέτρον, why cannot περὶ have the same construction and meaning as in the next clause and in Sym. 203, C. and Epist. ii. 312, E.; and even granting for argument sake, that the Epistles are not

NOTES.   187

Note ¹¹, p. 157.—The circular skull typifies noetic activity, the principle of Limitation; and the oblong body, the Indefinite. The triple soul of the Republic is psychological, while the single soul of the Phædo is metaphysical. Mr. Grote is of opinion that the Symposium recognises a metaphorical immortality only, ιι. p. 223. But Plato is speaking of ἡ θνητὴ φύσις, 207, D.; cf. ταύτῃ τῇ μηχανῇ (sc. γενέσει) θνητὸν ἀθανασίας μετέχει καὶ σῶμα καὶ τἆ- λλα· ἀθάνατον δὲ ἄλλῃ, 208, B. The passage cited from The Two Voices gives, it is conceived, the true sense of the Platonic Lethe considered as a state (λεληθέναι), and not as λήθης γένεσις; vide Phileb. 33, E.

Note ¹², (ib.)—Rep. x. 611, A.; cf. the declaration of the Demiurge, Tim. 41, A. D.; and ψυχὰς ἰσαρίθμους τοῖς ἄστροις, ib. D. That is, The Good is as the Sun (according to Philolaus), and inferior existences are consequently as the Stars.

Plato's (of which, however, there is no proof, vide Grote, I., p. 220), they at all events show the use of περὶ to denote the id circa quod of anything. The word ᾑρῆσθαι expresses exactly, choice determined by proper grounds, in which case the thing chosen is logically prior to the chooser. Besides, ᾑρῆσθαι need not, and must not be taken in the sense of either παρειληφέναι or εἰληχέναι. If we recollect Plato's use of ὀρέγεσθαι, Phæd. 65, C.; 75, A.; Rep. 572, A.; Epist. II. 312, E.; and Aristotle's objection to applying ἐφίεσθαι and ὄρεξις to the Numbers, Ethic. End. I. 8, we shall not only see no difficulty, but perfect propriety in the use of the word to express the complete harmony and distinctness of the elements of The Idea. Then, again, as the perfect tense signifies past and present time, it is the proper one to denote the non-transitional nature of The Idea. The reading suggested by Dr. Badham and by Professor W. H. Thompson, εὑρῆσθαι, would refer to the process of search, and not to the nature of the thing sought; but the previous discussion turned altogether on the latter point, Phil. 68. Finally, Plato, it is conceived, finds the Bonum most akin to Good in The Idea; for the Good is unknowable; but this is the doctrine of the Republic, vi. 509. A.; vii. 517, B. C. For these reasons, it is submitted that the reading of the Bodleian MS., ὁπόσα χρὴ ᾑρῆσθαι, κ. τ. λ. is right, or, if transposition be preferred, that the sense remains unaltered, but in no case need ᾑρῆσθαι be touched. We have a phrase of a similar kind in the Philebus itself, ὡς ἀγαθά μὲν οὐκ ὄντα, ἐνίοτε δὲ καὶ ἵνα διχόμενα τὴν τῶν ἀγαθῶν ἐστιν ὅτι φύσιν 82, D. Δέχεσθαι is, as the sense requires less strong, but the general notion is the same—of two things, and of a relation between them.

THE END.

www.ingramcontent.com/pod-product-compliance
Lightning Source LLC
Chambersburg PA
CBHW020933230426
43666CB00008B/1664